In a Chinese Garden

of the Dr. Sun Yat-Sen Classical Chinese Garden

AUTHORS

Maggie Keswick

Judy Oberlander

Joe Wai

PHOTOGRAPHERS

James Dow

James Jardine

Brian Mulvihill

The Dr. Sun Yat-Sen Garden Society of Vancouver

Cover and text design by Vic Marks
Typesetting by The Typeworks

The Dr. Sun Yat-Sen Classical Chinese Garden is the first authentic Ming dynasty-style Chinese garden built outside of China. Its financing and construction represent a unique co-operative effort between Canada and the People's Republic of China. The mandate of the Garden Society is to act as a cross-cultural bridge for greater understanding of the Chinese culture through developing quality educational and special event programs.

The Garden Society is a registered, non-profit society administered by a Board of Directors on behalf of the City of Vancouver.

Membership to the Garden can be obtained through writing to the:

Dr. Sun Yat-Sen Classical Chinese Garden
578 Carrall Street
Vancouver, B.C.
V6B 2J8
Tel. (604) 662-3207

Canadian cataloguing in publication data
Keswick, Maggie
"In a Chinese Garden: Its Art and Architecture; Dr. Sun Yat-Sen Classical Chinese Garden"
ISBN 0-9694573-0-8
1. Dr. Sun Yat-Sen Classical Chinese Garden (Vancouver, B.C.) 2. Gardens, Chinese—Art; 3. Landscape Architecture; I. Oberlander, Judy; II. Wai, Joe 1940 – ; III. Dr. Sun Yat-Sen Garden Society of Vancouver; IV. Title
SB 446.C33D7 1990 712é.5é0971133 C90-090382-1

PHOTOPLATE CREDITS

We wish to acknowledge the following individuals and institutions who have kindly given permission to reprint the material on the indicated pages:

His Excellency An Wenbin, Consul General of the Republic of China. pg. 63. Art Gallery of Greater Victoria.—1. Zhang Shibao. (1805 - 1879) "Courtyard Scene"; ink and colour on silk; 38.5 x 63.4 cm. Gift of J.P.E. Klaverwyden. pg. 8, 2. Zhu Melcun (1911 -) "Women in Thought"; ink and colour on paper; 111.8 x 26.2 cm. Collection of Brian S. McElney. pg. 11, 3. Feng Chaosan (1881/2 - 1954) "Rock and Fungus"; ink and colour on paper; 73.2 x 34 cm. Collection of Brian S. McElney. pg. 53. Cahill, James. Dept. of Fine Arts, University of California-Berkeley,—1. Chang Hung (1627) "Chih Garden" pg. 48. Tsu, Francis Ya-Sing. "Landscape Design in Chinese Gardens". Drawing adapted pg. 61. Joe Wai, Architect. inside cover, pg. 15, 47, 49, 64. Wu Yee-Sun. Hong Kong. pg. 58, 59, 60.

PHOTOGRAPH CREDITS

We wish to give special acknowledgement to the following photographers whose talents have contributed so much to this book:

Andrew Clunas, pg. 17, 33. James Dow, cover, pg. 28, 29 (bottom), 30-31, 41, 45. James Jardine, pg. 20, 22-23, 25, 26-27, 29 (bottom), 31 (top), 32, 33 (top), 35, 36, 37, 45, 56, 57. Michael Morrisette, pg. 52, 54. Bryan J. Mulvihill, pg. 3, 4, 5, 6, 7, 9, 19, 13, 21, 29 (top), 33 (bottom), 38, 39, 40, 41, 42, 44. Fiona Sinclair, 3,5. Don Vaughan, pg. 55. John Wong, pg. 46 and back cover.

I especially wish to recognize the effort of June McKenzie, my co-editor. Her depth of knowledge, enthusiasm, and support have been integral to the realization of this project. The Book Committee reached into the community and drew upon the expertise of many who generously gave of their time and advice—
Mr. Allan Bennett
Mrs. Terry Clark
Mr. Sidney Chan
Mrs. Ann Cherniavsky
Mr. Roy Forster
Mr. Glenn Hyatt
Mr. Allan MacDougall
Mr. Victor Marks
Mrs. Sarah McAlpine
Mrs. June McKenzie
Ms. Judy Oberlander
Mr. Barry Till
Mrs. Lynne Upton
I would like to particularly thank Roland Yu, Director of the Dr. Sun Yat-Sen Garden, Michael Patterson, Education Co-ordinator and Cecilia Ma, Secretary.

Joyce Pearkes
Project Chairman

Contents

Foreword

Enjoyment of a Chinese classical garden can be enhanced enormously if one attempts to understand the philosophy of its design.

In much earlier times, Chinese classical gardens were created in large measure for wealthy merchants who, though scholarly and cultured, did not wish to appear ostentatious. Gardens were created with elements designed to reflect the beauty of nature and to achieve a tranquil atmosphere. High walls were erected to isolate the pressures and distractions of the outside world, while strategically placed 'leak windows' admitted light, but not outside views.

The result of this now classic design is an atmosphere conducive to scholarly reflection and quiet meditation. Often in solitude, but occasionally with one or two scholars, the owner would walk the garden in leisurely fashion, delighting in the man-made rockeries and ponds, refreshing his mind and 'cleansing' from it the mundane concerns of commerce. Thus freed, his mind could turn to matters of philosophy and truth.

These intellectual reflections were frequently based on the teachings of Lao Zi, a 6th century B.C. contemporary of Confucius, and were concerned with the spiritual level of being. Lao Zi said "in the pursuit of earthly learning, as more knowledge is acquired, something is added to your mind; however, in the pursuit of spiritual learning, as more is learned, something is subtracted." The 'something' is bias, prejudice and the rigidities ingrained before the pursuit of spiritual learning was undertaken. As more and more is subtracted, the individual may find that these negative influences, these set ways of doing things and living one's life, have diminished, or even disappeared entirely, leaving one in a state of 'nothingness.' In that state, one may become totally free to pursue or achieve almost anything.

A quiet stroll in a Chinese classical garden, carefully exploring its beauties with an open philosophical mind, is a step toward achieving this beneficial state of 'nothingness.'

Enjoy this beautiful garden! Return as often as possible. Immerse yourself in the quiet beauty that only nature can provide, through meditation and the learning which results. May you achieve Lao Zi's state of total freedom!

David C. Lam
LIEUTENANT-GOVERNOR OF BRITISH COLUMBIA

Introduction

Chinese gardens are not like Western gardens—they need interpretation. Here, in the Dr. Sun Yat-Sen Classical Chinese Garden, informed guides are provided to lead the visitor through the intricacies of this ancient art form. Perhaps, however, there should be another way to experience the Garden—one which would allow a more personal pace and the pursuit of individual interests.

The eye of the botanist or gardener searches out the delicate bamboo, the gnarled pine and the winter-flowering plum. The historian reflects on the past as symbolized by plants and buildings which are the living exhibit of an ancient dynasty. The architect marvels at the exquisite and authentic details of the Garden construction. The philosopher, entering an oasis of calm in the Scholar's Courtyard, is transported to another realm of thought. The artist sees beauty in every element of the Garden and is moved by the effect of the changing seasons and the play of light on the plants, structures, rocks and water.

In order to interpret this beautiful Garden, our Board of Directors decided to publish a book which would include a comprehensive walking tour. Out of this mandate arose the need to place the Dr. Sun Yat-Sen Garden within its historical context, both past and present.

Maggie Keswick, the preeminent authority on Chinese Gardens, was asked to write an introduction for the book and, to our delight, sent her essay which became Chapter 1. Her lyrical prose exactly captures the essence of Chinese gardens. We welcomed her visit in 1987, and her enthusiasm and support for this Garden continues to be an inspiration to us.

Joe Wai, the architect of the Dr. Sun Yat-Sen Garden, and Don Vaughan, its landscape architect, also have contributed enormously to this publication. In Chapter 4, Joe Wai describes how the Garden came into being. His words give an immediacy to the story which could only have come from his authorship.

Judy Oberlander, retained to write the book, has woven a tapestry of individual experiences. Her contribution has been fundamental to furthering and interpreting the ideas of many in order to tell the story of Vancouver's 'living treasure'.

Joyce Pearkes
CHAIRMAN, BOOK COMMITTEE

Refreshment for the Heart

BY MAGGIE KESWICK

Among the great gardening civilizations of the world, China is something of a Cinderella, for it was not until the opening of China to tourism in the 1970s that foreigners first discovered the old private gardens of China's traditional elite – and with them an ancient, unbroken tradition of gardening very different from their own.

Perhaps this is not surprising. Chinese gardens are based on a deep appreciation of the natural landscape – but what is seen as 'natural' in one culture can sometimes look strangely artificial in another. Of the three main types of gardens developed in China, the 'naturalness' of the first two is quite straightforward: in the great imperial parks, for instance, palace and temple complexes seem set, apparently at random, among naturally formed hills and serpentine lakes (although in fact these are often as man-made as the palaces). The second type – public parks in areas of unusual beauty – actually *are* 'natural', since it is the art of locating a site, building little open-sided viewing pavilions, making them accessible by paths and carving on the living rock calligraphic inscriptions to inspire the visitor that turns the chosen landscape into a *jardin trouvé*.

The third type, however, is more difficult – and more interesting. The old private gardens of China's traditional elite were seldom seen by foreigners in the past and, when seen, usually dismissed. Characteristically in dense, urban sites, they are in essence secret gardens whose high, white walls separate the bustling city from the peace of nature within. For those seeing them for the first time, however, the Chinese conviction that these gardens are as 'natural' as the others (especially as opposed to the 'artificial' gardens of Japan) may come as a surprise.

Firstly, they seem to be almost all architecture – mazes of walls within walls, with courtyards wrapped round still smaller courtyards, while an astonishing number and variety of pavilions, halls, bridges, covered galleries and summer-houses crowd in on the viewer. Trees and flowers play a relatively minor role. There is nothing even remotely like a lawn and, although the small lakes and streams seem to follow 'natural' courses, they are surrounded by extraordinary rocks which, both singly and in huge piles, often dominate the scene. Moreover, compared to the elegant rocks of Japanese gardens, rocks seen in Chinese gardens seem almost grotesque, enormous piles looming twelve feet high above the walls and running wild along the lake shores. The visitor's eyes move restlessly over their fragmented shapes, seeking a place to rest. The effect, far from the contemplative stillness of Zen stone gardens, is almost violently energetic.

▲ *The spirit of a classical garden filled with people is captured in this hanging scroll, "Courtyard Scene".*

Not in his wildest dreams would a Westerner describe such rocks as 'natural': to understand how the Chinese came to see them so, it is necessary to know something of their history, and of the complex and multilayered ideas about natural forces that lie behind them.

Nature, 'Vital Breath' and the Feng Shui Masters

The Chinese attitude to nature is an amalgam of ideas and feelings which spill over from magic into philosophy and from spirituality into aesthetics and the arts. A key is that in prehistoric times, great landscape features – mountains, hills and even large or strangely-shaped rocks – were felt to be imbued with supernatural power. By the 5th century B.C. we have a poem from the *Songs of Chu* that already expresses, in words of passionate terror and awe, the numinous beauty of mountain peaks and chasms. In the West such scenes would come to represent the chaos from which God's divine love would rescue man: not until the 15th century A.D. did Petrarch become the first European to record climbing a mountain for the sheer exhilaration of its beauty – and he was tormented by guilt lest this material ravishment draw his soul from God.

Unencumbered by the Western split between body and soul, the Chinese held that everything in existence is composed of the same fundamental *qi*, a 'Vital Breath' which pulses through nature in different degrees of intensity, in 'dragon veins' or currents of energizing force.

The dancing dragons of Chinese art represent the energy of this *qi* as it moves through and vitalizes all living matter. From deep in the heart of mountain peaks (the dragon's lair) it rises along the 'dragon's back' and cascades to the valleys below until, growing ever heavier and more earthy, it winds in sluggish streams to the sea. Thence, drawn up by heaven, it leaps again and lightens, swirling amongst the clouds to descend, revitalized and pure, as rain upon the mountain peaks. In this endless cycle, where the polar opposites of *yin* and *yang* are

▶ *Not in his wildest dreams would a Westerner describe such rocks as natural, but the Chinese accept them as such.*

represented in their most extreme phases by the surging power of oceans (*yin*) and the translucent *yang* energy of the sky, man stands midway, a blend of both, united by the Vital Breath with everything else in existence.

The courses of *qi*, which can be traced both in the physical features and in the orientation of a landscape, exert a powerful effect on human affairs, since those families prosper who place their houses – and in particular the graves of their ancestors – in propitious, well-veined sites; those who do not may fail. In the 3rd century A.D. the practice of Chinese geomancy by *feng shui* masters skilled in the location and manipulation of *qi* was already so important that the biography of Qu Yuan, an early expert, was included in one of China's earliest literary collections. Pools and terraces built by China's earlier, mythical kings may have had geomantic as well as ritual significance while, later, the lakes of the Han emperors were held to concentrate beneficent forces. In the 12th century Emperor Hui Tsung justified building his gigantic rock garden, Gen Yu, near Loyang, as necessary *feng shui* because the throne lacked heirs.

Since *qi* waxes, wanes, alters course and is affected by any change to the topography, *feng shui* masters have advised – at least since the 3rd century A.D. – not only on the siting of new buildings in China, but on remedial actions such as planting trees, building walls, relocating furniture and hanging mirrors to deflect *sha*, the straight-flying 'arrows' of evil influence.

The principles of *feng shui* naturally also affected

Feng-shui masters plot the earth's currents of energizing force (qi).

the location of gardens and the placing of pavilions, lakes and rocks within them. Even more influential, however, was an alluring promise it held out – that of longevity.

Vital Breath and the Preservation of Youth

From very early times the Chinese, never much given to speculations on an afterlife, were obsessed by the prolongation of youthful energies. Many folk tales involved the *hsien*, or Chinese Immortals, who dissolve in the air, travel on the wind, and fly about on the backs of storks. They live either in the Kunlun Mountains – the axis of the world and a kind of lightning conductor for *qi* at its most *yang* – or on movable islands in that vast repository of *yin* energy, the Eastern Sea. Qin Shi Huang (the Emperor whose terracotta armies lie buried near Xian a round his tomb) once hoped to discover the Immortals' secrets by sending an expedition to these islands, but although visible from a distance, they vanished into the mist like the *hsien* themselves once ships approached. Later the Han Emperor Wudi tried instead to bring the *hsien* to him by building a great lake behind his palace with islands in it so beautiful the Immortals would mistake them for their own. Oddly, though he died in normal old age, he did achieve a kind of immortality, since it is an echo of that ancient lake-and-island pattern visitors still enjoy in gardens all over China and Japan today.

Many Daoist searchers for immortality set out to emulate the *hsien* by finding the secrets of longevity for themselves, seeking at first a perfect balance of *yin* and *yang* forces, and an absolute unity with all created things. One of the Seven Sages of the Bamboo Grove, having achieved this ultimate oneness, sat naked in his room and, when visitors complained, answered: "The whole world is my house and my room, my clothing. Why then do you enter here into my trousers?"

Nature and Daoism

Contemplation of nature can trigger this latent sense of unity: a man who stands in the spring snow gazing intently into a cloud of plum blossom may suddenly feel his heart unfold, as if it too were flowering – and thus, through nature, experience the mysterious oneness of the *Dao.*

Through breathing exercises, diet and sexual techniques these adepts sought to control the movement of *qi* through their bodies so as to become one with the eternal currents of time and change they called the *Dao.* For those who were successful, youth might be prolonged indefinitely and death at last would be no more fearful than drawing breath. Others still sought a potion of long life to put off this inevitable event. By including mercury as a necessary ingredient, often they died in the attempt. Others wandered into the hills looking for the magic *lung chieh* mushrooms of immortality. And they also sought, by locating those parts of the landscape with the greatest concentrations of *qi*, to saturate themselves in its vital, invigorating forces.

Nature Poetry

As they wandered, many of these longevity-seekers also found that the grandeur of the landscape itself had an effect as it distanced them from the inconsequential cares of man. The phrase 'longing for mountains and waters' became synonymous with the life of the spirit. One great official of the third century A.D., asked his opinion of a new prime minister, replied: "In official matters I am no better, but in appreciation of hills and waters I think I surpass him."

In the fourth century A.D., Tao Yuanming became the first great poet to crystallize this link, and to give lyric form to the ideal of the cultivated man retreat-

The Garden is a contemplative world. "Women in Thought" by Zhu Melcun.

ing from "the web of the world's dust" back to nature. Released from a job he loathed, he wrote,

> "I lean on the southern window and let my pride
>   expand
> I consider how easy it is to be content with a small
>   space
> Everyday I stroll in the garden for pleasure . . .
> And walk round my lonely pine tree, stroking it."

Even today, when Chinese poets speak of woods and mountains they are implying (though by now it is a fairly worn convention) not just a physical or emotional need, but a spiritual one.

Buddhism and Nature

Buddhism, which gradually filtered into China from India, also made use of this indigenous idea. Monasteries were sited – as we see them in a thousand landscape paintings – high in the hills, their upturned roofs echoing the swoops and hollows of the crags around them; below, the soundless, misty depths of valleys became symbols of the Void. Monastery gardens also preserved old trees (notable repositories of *qi*) – something impossible elsewhere in a country starved of fuel. Natural landscape parks were probably begun by Buddhist monks who, returning in the fourth century A.D. from the great monastery on Lu Shan mountain, tried to recreate the peace and majesty of its setting in the form of 'Lu Shan parks', open to the public, but in reach of their home cities.

Buddhist laymen also sometimes sought retreat in country estates. The most famous of these, lying along the Wang River some thirty miles north of the Tang capital at Changan, was made by Wang Wei (A.D. 701-761), an artist, calligrapher, musician and poet. The scroll painting and poems he made of his Wang Chuan Villa were endlessly copied and recopied down the years, not only because of the physical charm of the villa's gentle hills and pavilions, nor even because of delicacy and brilliance of the scroll itself, but because the character of the man who made it imbued the garden – and his painting – with a profound and tranquil feeling of erudition and spirituality. In the words of the modern historian Wango Weng, this is what "every Chinese scholar since would like to re-create around him."

In China, however, it was not always easy to take off for the hills, abandoning family, friends and civic duties – not least because essential Confucian duties were filial piety and marriage, both necessary for the continued performance of ancestral rites. Surprisingly perhaps, this too had great implications for gardening.

The Confucian Aspect

It has been said that the Chinese used to be Confucian in office, Daoist out of it and Buddhist in death. While the Daoist Lao Zi concerned himself with man in nature, and Buddhists tried to remove themselves from earthly desires, Confucius concentrated on the relationship between man and man and the rites and duties of a well-balanced society. In particular Confucius' followers emphasized the necessity for an ethical man to render service to the state and, in the Han dynasty (220 B.C. – 206 B.C.), Confucian teachings, somewhat adapted, became state orthodoxy. For approximately the next two thousand years stringent imperial examinations in the Chinese classics weeded out the unworthy and filled civil-service posts across the land with a highly cultivated and extensively educated elite.

Gardening was affected, since only the rich had time for gardens and, in traditional China, a position in the mandarinate was the only acceptable route to wealth and success. Families exerted the greatest possible pressure on sons who were potential candidates; and a man of promise who endangered his prospects by taking to the hills – however great his spiritual longings – was unlikely to be commended for filial piety. Once in office it was hard to escape.

The solution lay in recreating nature near at hand. Pavilions in the countryside could provide summer accommodation within an acceptable distance of civilization while preserving the illusion of escape. However, as one scholar-official remarked, "if the heart is at peace, why should one not create a wilderness even in the midst of town?" A high wall could exclude the activities of men, while the inside is returned to nature. Here, in the company of a few like-minded friends and a jar of wine, the harassed official could both assuage his longing for mountains and waters and saturate his weary body in currents of life-enhancing *qi* – while still fulfilling his duties to state and family. The Buddhist Vimalakirti, a man who despite wife and children, once had achieved Nirvana by remaining "unmoved in the midst of movement," reinforced the appeal of gardens. Not only the owner but all his family could benefit from the channelling of Vital Force which a garden made possible.

On Reduction and Concentration

What Chinese garden-makers aimed at, behind their high white walls, was not merely to represent or copy parts of nature on a smaller scale but to create, within a small space, a total landscape with all the forms of lakes and mountains, rocks, old trees, streams, hills and valleys – and, above all, the *qi* that animated them. It is an idea that goes back to Emperor Qin Shi Huang who, after uniting the ancient Chinese kingdoms in 221 BC, replicated the palaces of the conquered kings in miniature around his capital. As further proof of his supremacy, he also collected tribute of rare animals and vegetation from every corner of his new empire for the Shang-lin park north of the city. The Han emperors who followed him knew a potent symbol when they saw one; they retained and added to the parks and set the great prose-poets of their time to immortalize them. It is in the fantastic descriptions of these poems, in which magic and reality fuse to create a mythic portrait of the empire in miniature, that the garden first becomes more than a pleasing adornment – more even than a symbolic collection of the riches, variety and beauty of the earth, becomes, in fact, a microcosm where the miniaturization of

Huge rocks may be set up much as sculpture is in a Western garden.

living forms concentrates and makes even more perfect the powerful forces of nature.

The most extreme examples of this belief in the power of reduction are those small bowl landscapes, *penjing*, or Chinese bonsai, found not only in garden courtyards, on scholars' desks and in summerhouses, but before the main halls of temples. They are afforded these places of honour because, not unlike cooking stock boiled down to increase its flavour, the great reduction in their size concentrates the Vital Force within them. To dwarf a tree it was thought necessary to 'slow down the sap', much as the Hsien Daoist's respiratory exercises slowed the journey of breath round his body. For both, the technique was to twist and stretch the limbs. The little trees, which grew into strange contorted shapes, soon seemed immeasurably old yet full of life and vigour, while the gardener who trained them reaped, by a kind of sympathetic magic, the rejuvenating benefits of their concentrated *qi*.

Rocks and Water

Equally effective miniaturizations are the great stones and piled-up rockeries unique to Chinese gardens. Famous collections of mineral stones were first recorded in the Tang dynasty, perhaps fascinating their owners by the traces they still showed of the formidable telluric energies which had created them. Huge single rocks, *shi feng*, may be set up much as sculpture is in Western gardens, on plinths in courtyards. The most famous of these stones are of water-worn limestone *(taihu shi)* from Lake Tai, near Shanghai. During the Song dynasty, they were the most expensive objects in the empire. Both muscular and delicate, they rise from their narrowest points. From the front – the south or *yang* side

– their flanks swoop out in curves, holes and hollows like frozen clouds; from the back – the north or *yin* side – they are often much straighter, their texture rougher, greyer, scraped with fissures. Potent harmonies of polar opposites, they can be seen as concentrations of China's five sacred mountains and as axis-of-the-world stones.

The tiny slivers of space behind or between buildings in Chinese gardens are often enlivened with compositions of three such rocks, placed to simulate a range of peaks, like the Chinese character for 'mountain', against the whitewashed background of a wall.

Above all, however, there are the 'false mountains', or *jia shan*, which so confused early Western travellers: huge piles of pitted rocks held together by invisible wires, cement and the garden-maker's competence in dynamic equilibrium. Sometimes they are hollowed into rough caves for summer shade, sometimes planted with trees and smoothed with earthy banks, and sometimes made into three-dimensional labyrinths wound round with little paths and steps leading up to belvederes.

Such rocks, combined with streams and pools, form the basis of a garden's plan. The Chinese word for landscape, *shan shui*, literally means 'mountains and waters' while a common phrase for making (in English we would say planting) a garden means 'digging ponds and piling mountains'. In nature, mountains are the skeleton of the earth and streams its arteries; in a garden, rocks form the bony structure, water its living pulse. The rocks are hard, unmoving, masculine and *yang*, and they must harmonize and balance the reflective, flowing *yin* of water. But since *yin* forever gives way to *yang*, and *yang* to *yin* in the unceasing pendulum of change, on sunny days when light sparkles off the water and shimmering leaves cast shadows on these tormented heaps, it may often seem as if it is the rocks that move, the water that is motionless.

Often Chinese visitors like to point out faces and the figures of animals – lions, eagles, tortoises, deer – which come into focus as the sun moves round the rocks. In Qing gardens, made often not by the literati but by *nouveaux riches* merchants, this can become an obsession, obscuring the subtle play on what is 'real' and 'unreal' in a vulgar display of too-obvious animal rock forms. Even in late and vulgar gardens, however, more aware visitors may trace the flow of *qi* from the high peaks down twisting gullies to the 'sea' of the central lake. And they will feel, too, the benevolent forces collected round the various pavilions and halls.

Architecture in Gardens

"Once we have a *ting* (pavilion)" one saying goes, "we can say we have a garden." Chinese scholars divide their gardens into two types, strolling and fixed-point, but many, especially imperial and nature gardens, are both, with paths that wind among continuously changing scenes, up hills and along the lake shores to stop momentarily at a set piece framed in the pillars of a *ting*.

Even relatively small examples of old private gardens, like the beautiful one-acre *Wang Shi Yuan* (Garden of the Master of the Fishing Nets) in Suzhou, manage both types of viewing – but not, however, at speed. These places, after all, were made to be savoured over a lifetime (and they often took a lifetime to make.) For a woman with bound feet, her family garden (if she were lucky enough to have one) might be virtually her whole experience of nature. Small wonder if tourists, whisked through three Suzhou gardens in an afternoon, get visual indigestion.

Pavilions and Summerhouses

In the garden-maker's repertoire there are at least ten different types of pavilion: two-storied *lou* or *ge* that give long views and 'borrow' scenery from outside the garden walls; ceremonial halls (*tang*, *ting*) which were the first to be placed in a new garden; extended porches for sitting in (*xuan*); little gazebos (*xie*); summerhouse-in-the-shape-of-a-boat (*fang*); the studios, studies and libraries without which no garden is worthy of the name, and the open-sided (*ting*) which both focuses (from a distance) and frames (when inside it) the landscape all around.

All these buildings are in some measure enclosed, sometimes tightly, in courtyards, sometimes inter-

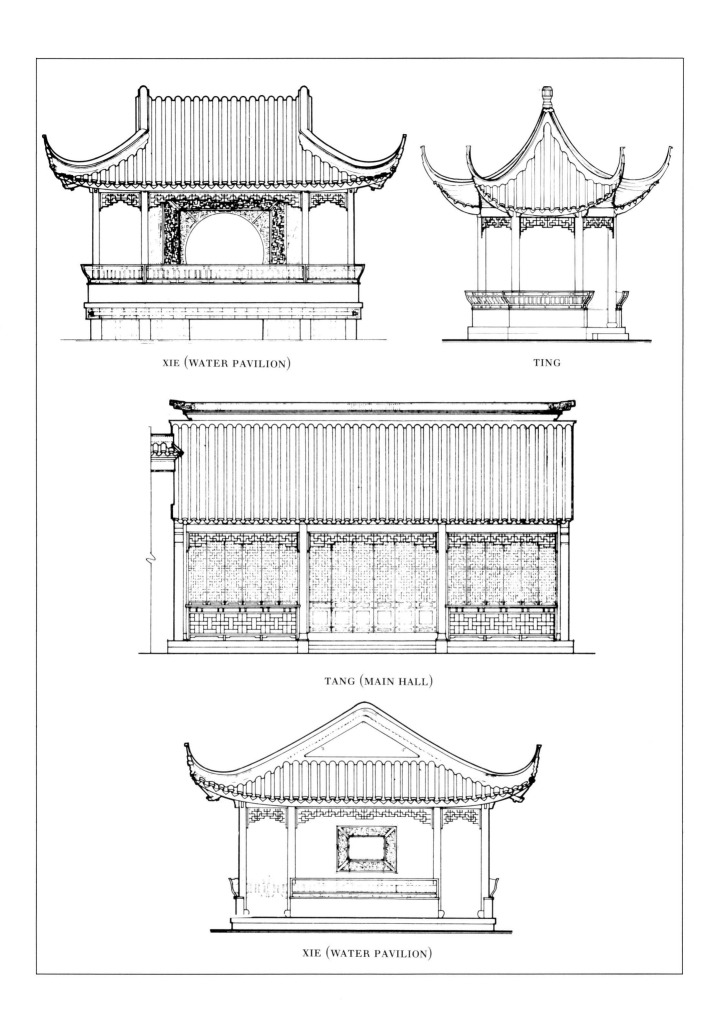

XIE (WATER PAVILION)

TING

TANG (MAIN HALL)

XIE (WATER PAVILION)

locked with each other, sometimes in much larger spaces whose walls vanish out of sight behind hills, trees and other buildings. The garden's boundary walls are tall and whitewashed, occasionally opened with fretwork *lou chuang* windows made of tiles. Placed high, these windows let in sunlight without allowing precious Vital Force to leak away. Inside the garden, walls twist and zigzag, their grey-tiled roofs sometimes undulating in regular waves like sea snakes or dragons. They order the currents of *qi*, channelling it round the halls and sitting-terraces, containing it in courtyards, and allowing it to spill from one enclosed space to another through many window openings. Here these are often in propitious or humorous shapes like bells, teacups, pomegranates, banana trees or vases – these last a play on sounds since the word for 'vase', *ping*, is a homonym for 'peace'. Moon gates, often used as entrances to gardens, likewise use the symbolism of the circle, suggesting 'heaven' and 'perfection'.

Once inside, *lang*, or roofed and open-sided galleries, make it possible to walk to all parts of the garden whatever the weather. They zigzag in irregular turns along walls, across open spaces and, metamorphosing into verandahs, round formal halls. Bridges also sometimes zigzag across the lakes, always an uneven number of times to shake off the straight-flying currents of *sha*. But they may also take the visitor low over the water on flat stone slabs, or raise him high above a stream to give a new perspective and reflection.

Trees, shrubs and flowers

The layering of all these buildings is enhanced and made more mysterious by planting, for the visitor is lured on through the maze of courtyards not only by the promise of another charming pavilion, its top just visible above the further wall but also, perhaps, the sudden flash of blossom, backlit in sunshine, through an opening.

Unlike Europeans, the Chinese did not particularly seek novelty in horticulture, preferring plants rich not only in physical beauty but in historical, literary and symbolic associations. Since more than 2000 miles separate the northern gardens of Beijing from those of the subtropical south, the consistency of these associations is remarkable. *Sophora japonica*, the 'scholar's tree', for instance, is placed whenever possible by studies and libraries. Bananas, loved for the sound of rain pattering on their leaves, are grown far into the north, padded in winter with straw jackets. Pomegranates, symbols of fertility because of their multitudinous seeds, are pot-grown in Beijing and moved to sheltered quarters in October.

The traditional matching of flowers with seasons may vary. *Nelumbium speciosum*, the pink lotus of Buddhist legend, are sometimes replaced as the flower of northern summers by peonies; in the south these are the flower of spring. And while the orchard trees of the north are apples, pears, cherries and persimmon, in the far south they are citrus, loquat and lichee.

Nevertheless, orchids are everywhere the symbol of a gentleman, since their scent, though exquisite, is so unassertive it often goes unnoticed till visitors miss it by its absence. Chrysanthemums, China's oldest cultivated flower, are associated with long life, and bamboos with an honourable man who bends, yet does not break. Willows, their supple branches reminiscent of dancing girls, suggested easy virtue: as a result (and despite willow-patterned plates), though planted against the red walls of the Forbidden City and as street trees in the water-cities of the south, willows are not found in gardens near women's apartments.

Other popular trees are pawlonias in the north, cassias, *Firmania simplex*, the *wu-tung* tree, legendary perch of the Chinese phoenix, and, in the south, frangipanis for their heady scent. Roses are grown on trellises, *moutan*, or tree peonies, in raised beds, these last so sought after in the Tang and Song dynasties that one rare bloom cost the lifetime wages of a labourer. Above all, however, what every Chinese longed for in his garden was an old pine tree, its trunk hoary and twisted with age, its glorious needles sighing in the breezes overhead. "Whence,"

▶ *The Chinese preferred plants rich not only in physical beauty, but in historical, literary and symbolic associations.*

asked one scholar, "are the joys of life to come, if one has not a pine tree and a jar of wine?"

Pines brought the dignity of age into the garden as well as their vigorous evergreen beauty, and pines, like the bamboos and winter plum associated with them as the 'three friends of winter', were also a constant motif in Chinese art. Almost all garden-makers were also painters, just as they were scholars, calligraphers and poets.

The Aesthetics of Gardens: Painting

Aesthetically, however, it is impossible to see a garden through Chinese eyes without having some appreciation of Chinese landscape painting.

"The question of reality will not really bother [the visitor]" says a twentieth-century Chinese, "as soon as he ceases to be in the *garden* and starts to live in the *painting*." Ji Cheng, who wrote China's first garden manual, the *Yuan Yeh*, in 1634 AD, maintained that his secret in building false mountains success-fully was not only to take the natural striations of the rocks into account, but to "follow cracks . . . imitat-ing the brushwork of old masters" as he linked the fissured boulders into a sculptural whole. By a com-bination of skill and the mellowing passage of time, "it need not be obvious that a mountain is artificial," for, "the buildings and terraces will grow to look like a painting." In other words, artificiality is a falsifica-tion not of 'nature', but of 'art,' and it is the truth of a work of art, not a mere reproduction of natural forms, that the garden-maker seeks.

When the Chinese looked at nature they saw it through eyes educated by a thousand years of land-scape painting. When they arranged rocks and bam-boo and their shifting shadows against a white-washed wall, that wall became the equivalent of empty silk, the background of a landscape scroll. In certain lights – at dawn or dusk, or the blinding glare of summer noon – it might even seem to have melted away altogether, leaving the rocks and bam-boo floating in the horizonless and vaporous dis-tances of a Song painting. Shrinking himself in imagination to the size of an ant, the connoisseur could wander in these misty wastes among rocks now grown into mountains, and shrubs and grasses

as big as trees and forests. And as he walked and paused, the landscape unfolded around him as if he were taking a three-dimensional stroll through one of his own paintings, slowly unrolling the horizontal scroll from right to left. Thus he could create a para-dox in the garden: for the walls that enclosed and limited his space also served to extend it magically beyond all bounds.

As painters and connoisseurs, these men would also, however unconsciously, in gardens as in art, have looked for a quality described as *qi yun sheng tong*. This, the 'first principle' of painting, was for-mulated by Xie He in the sixth century A.D. and has been interpretatively developed by others ever since. Translated by Alexander Soper as "animation through spirit consonance," it means two things: first, that the *qi* of every part of a painting must 'vibrate' with the *qi* of every other part; second, that the *qi* of the painted forms must respond to that of the real forms as they exist outside the painting. In aesthetic terms it thus implies both inner con-sistency, by which themes set up harmonious vi-brations among themselves, and a mystical real-ism, whereby the artist magically captures the animating spirit of nature itself. Thus trained, the garden designer also seeks the essence behind the forms – the *energies* of mountains rather than the shape of a specific range – and feels the special qual-ities of his site, allowing them to lead him to the reality of art. Much will depend on his own qualities for, as Ji Cheng says, "When you have the real thing within you, it will become real." In the end the gar-den-maker will 'know that it is right when it moves him.'

And this, perhaps, is the key; for within its own small space a garden must make possible a whole range of emotions that otherwise could be felt only in nature. Thus the garden designer strives to heighten his effects by contrast and juxtaposition – high leading to low, open to closed, narrow to wide, light to dark – in a constant, delicate pairing, on an infinity of levels, that echoes the dynamic equilib-rium of *yin* and *yang*. In practice the designer man-ages so to confuse the visitor about how he came in, where he is and how he is to get out, and at the same time so to delight and lull his senses that the space of his little garden seems to extend indefinitely.

The Literary Dimension

It extends indefinitely also in a literary sense. Since Confucius had spent most of his life out of office, his ethics included an ideal of self-cultivation and relaxation through the arts, both to replenish an official's energy and to make best use of his time when unemployed. Gardens became an acceptable venue for writing poetry, practising calligraphy or admiring antiques, and the French phrase *cultiver son jardin* has added meaning in China.

For an educated Chinese, part of the pleasure of a garden lies in the savouring of *vers d'occasion* written by previous visitors and engraved on stone tablets let into the walls. Just as a great landscape painting acquires, over time, the calligraphy of connoisseurs as colophons around its margins, so the garden acquires history, life and meaning from poems that record the feelings of those who, maybe a hundred years before, enjoyed the same sights and sounds and scents as still are there today.

In addition, paired couplets were written in expressive calligraphy on each side of gateways, and the names of pavilions or courtyards on wooden tablets above their entrances. Choosing such names often provided a game in which scholars could cap each other with a brilliant literary allusion or an apt metaphor. They set the mood for each new part of the garden, probing layers of literary recollection, adding new insights to old meanings. And the supple and powerful strokes of the calligraphy in which they were written echoed the shapes of the leaves and branches.

Although the magical purposes of garden-making in China may seem to have been largely subsumed under centuries of skillful practice and aesthetic development, an atavistic sense of their power still persists. They are strangely moving places which, if we have time to listen, have much to tell us of man, and nature, and how we may grow in harmony together.

A Walk through the Garden

DR. SUN YAT-SEN
CLASSICAL CHINESE GARDEN

BY JUDY OBERLANDER

Surrounded by imposing, almost forbidding white walls, this classical Chinese garden beckons you. Above the narrow doorway is a plaque, *Yi Yuan* or 'Garden of Ease' – *Yi* meaning ease or tranquility and *Yuan* meaning garden or park. This plaque also commemorates the middle name of Dr. Sun Yat-Sen, the founder of modern China. It is here that you enter into a harmonious world filled with the delights of nature. The small narrow courtyard, the intricate pebble paving, soft bamboo and craggy rocks are a preview of the Garden – almost an overture – to what lies beyond.

A glimpse of the Garden can be seen through the leak window set high into the white wall. This is a selected or 'borrowed' view and a peek into the Garden. These views which create the impression of much larger spaces are characteristic of classical Chinese gardens. Past the narrow passageway you are drawn towards the light of the Central Courtyard. Here the Garden unfolds with a myriad of images – the craggy rocks, cloudy water ponds, delicate trees and shrubs, lattice screens, open colonnades and pavilions. Unable to absorb all these images at once, your attention is drawn from one area to another as you cast your eyes across the Central Courtyard.

This garden, like ones built in scholar's residences in Suzhou during the Ming dynasty (1368-1644 A.D.), is meant to be an expression of the natural landscape as filtered through the heart of the builder. This small site, approximately one-third of

◀ *The small narrow entrance is a preview of the garden – almost an overture.*

an acre, is characteristic of the private spaces which adjoined the scholars' residences. Its asymmetrical layout, with winding paths and corridors, rocks and plants, and vistas overlooking the courtyards is intended to capture the rhythm of nature. The Garden is an idealized version, or a microcosm, of the world outside its walls.

Standing at the entrance to the double corridor you can see much of the Garden. However, there is no vantage point from which a total view is possible. This is a deliberate part of a classical garden's design, since surprise and ever-changing views play an important role in the use of space. Small spaces are subdivided to give the impression of more. "In laying out garden pavilions and towers, suites of rooms and covered walkways, piling rocks into mountains, or planting flowers to form a desired shape, the aim is to see the small in the large, to see the large in the small, to see the real in the illusory and to see the illusory in the real."[1]

Selected or 'borrowed' views through open doorways and delicate lattice windows create the impression of much larger areas. The distinction between inside and out is blurred, and the effect is like a large outdoor room or an interior garden.

Part of the Garden's mystery is the way it evokes a sense of 'ease'. The tone of the Garden is set soon after you enter; the small sunken courtyard on the right as you wander through the corridor invites a detailed examination of the plants and intricate pebble floors. A ledge serves as a seat from which to contemplate the views – both static and dynamic – which unfold as you look across the courtyard.

The Main Hall

Here behind you is the Main Hall, known as *Hua Feng T'ang*, China Maple Hall, honouring friendship between Canada and China. This south-facing pavilion is the Garden's reception area, and was traditionally used as a formal living room in which the scholar would entertain his literati friends. Built by Suzhou artisans using traditional materials brought from China, and constructed with mortise and tenon, this Hall characterizes the type of buildings found in other Suzhou gardens. The high roof lined with camphor wood rafters rests on elegantly crafted pillars of prized Nan wood and lacquered Chinese fir. The delicate latticework screens are made of ginkgo wood.

Piercing the northern wall are three windows opening onto a shallow courtyard which give the impression of living pictures. Each one is composed like a painting set against the background of the white wall; plants — bamboo, pine, a camellia and a lily of the valley shrub — contrast with the rocks.

Just outside the Main Hall the plant materials have been carefully selected to reflect the interior materials. A Japanese red maple alludes to the name of the Main Hall and a ginkgo tree to the right echoes the latticework inside.

▶ *This south-facing pavilion was traditionally used as a formal living room where the scholar would entertain his literati friends.*

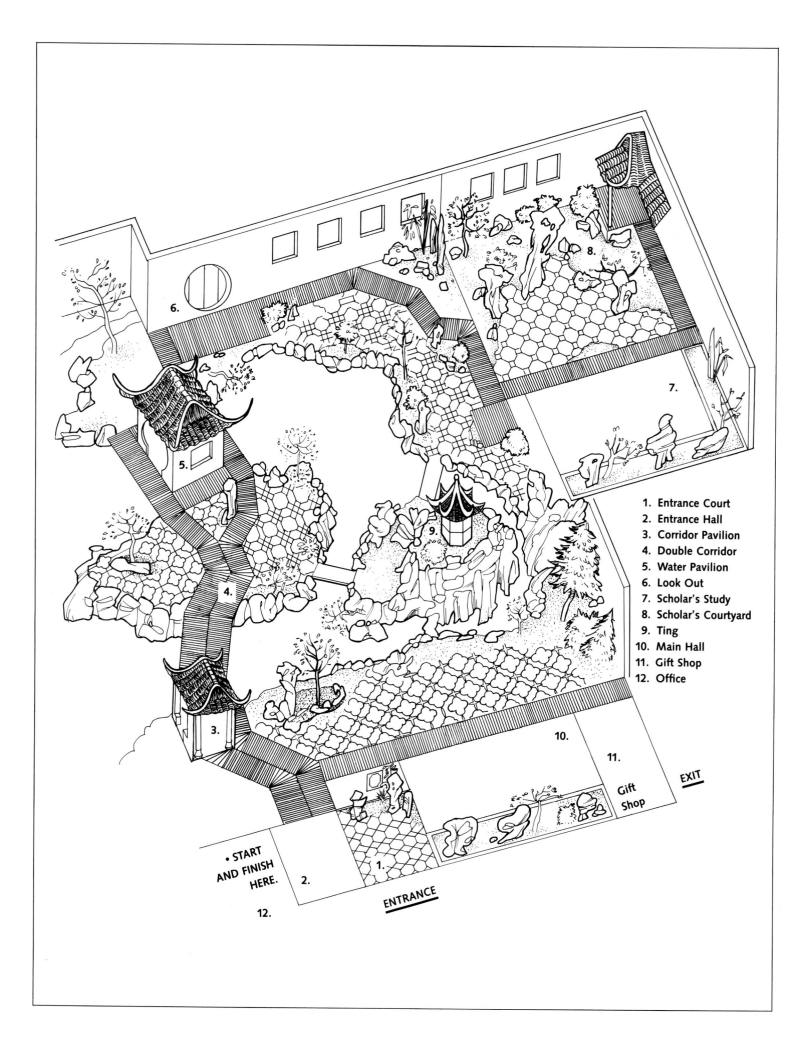

1. Entrance Court
2. Entrance Hall
3. Corridor Pavilion
4. Double Corridor
5. Water Pavilion
6. Look Out
7. Scholar's Study
8. Scholar's Courtyard
9. Ting
10. Main Hall
11. Gift Shop
12. Office

• START AND FINISH HERE.

ENTRANCE

EXIT

Gift Shop

The Central Courtyard

From the building's dark interior to the contrast of daylight, you arrive at the open, airy courtyard which forms the heart of the Garden. It expresses the essence of the Garden since landscape in Chinese, *shan shui*, translates as 'mountains and waters'. These two elements are the focus of the Central Courtyard; the craggy, precariously perched rocks of water-eroded limestone from China's Lake Tai create a solid mountain around which the cloudy waters flow. High upon this pile of weathered rocks sits an elegant pavilion, or *ting*, designed to represent man in his natural setting. Known as *Yun Wei Ting*, the Colourful and Cloudy Pavilion, it forms the focal point for the large rock formation and further reinforces the Daoist philosophy of *yin* and *yang* expressed by the massive and solid rocks juxtaposed with the gently moving ephemeral waters below. Omnipresent and mystical, these rocks are an integral part of the Garden landscape. Designed to emulate a mountain, these sinister and mysterious-looking rocks recall natural rock formations formed in China many centuries ago. They are piled high to evoke mountains or close together to create small caves; they define spaces within the Garden, serve as links between the cut stone steps and pebble mosaics, and form borders around the water ponds. Throughout the Garden, their sculptural quality creates the forceful imagery of a natural landscape.

These rock arrangements reflect Chinese aesthetics. Evocative of supernatural powers and mysterious beings, they draw us into another world. This is particularly evident in the grotto behind the *ting*. According to Chinese legend, mountains, islands and caves were mythical dwellings of the Immortals. By including them in his own garden, the scholar hoped to entice these 'good spirits' to dwell there.

Symbolism is an integral part of all classical gardens and it exists on many different levels. As a whole, the Garden represents the harmonious interaction between man and nature, and this is reflected in the architectural and natural elements of the Garden. You will notice that some of the steps between the corridors and the pebble courtyards are irregular Lake Tai rocks rather than refined granite blocks. This is intended to soften the man-made elements.

Similarly, this integration of man and nature is visible in the smooth granite planks of the bridges between the island and the shore, which contrast with the rugged rock formations.

Symbolism from the plant and animal worlds is also visible throughout the Garden. For example, floral motifs appear in the pebble floors, the wooden balustrades and leak windows. Animals are also used as symbols. The bronze door handles at the entrance to the pavilions are shaped like bats. This motif reappears in the roof tiles which can be seen throughout the Garden. In Chinese, bat is *pin fu*, which is a homonym meaning both 'bat' and 'good fortune'. Consequently, the bat is symbolic of good fortune.

The combination of traditional materials and the desire to selectively re-create vignettes of the natural world is part of an historical continuum steeped in Chinese mythology and mysticism. As a reflection of the natural landscape, gardens were therefore an extension of the natural world despite man's intervention.

The imagery of balanced opposites is the core of Daoist philosophy. Juxtaposing the *yang* (the solid, permanent, masculine) and the *yin* (the void, ephemeral, feminine) is a central part of classical garden design. This is visible at all levels from the

▶ *High upon the craggy, weathered rocks sits the Yun Wei Ting, the Colourful and Cloudy Pavilion, which represents man in this natural setting.*

combinations of materials to the intentional placement of contrasting elements side by side. Massive rocks emerge from gently flowing waters, lush grasses are placed next to the smooth pebbles of the courtyard floor, and bamboo branches brush against the rock 'bamboo shoots'; all are harmoniously combined in different parts of the Garden.

The rocks vividly illustrate contrasts between solid and void, light and dark, as well as open and closed, the known and the unknown. With time and weather, light changes their colour and a seemingly infinite palette of greys emerges. Rainwater splashing over the rocks alters their texture and over time, they become covered with moss and develop a beautiful greenish patina. This weathering effect adds to the rocks' natural beauty, providing the Garden with a sense of age which only occurs in nature.

Wandering along the pathways of the Central Courtyard, these bold, asymmetrical rocks appear to move. At times it is unsettling as you struggle to focus on them. New images emerge as your imagination takes over. Each visit inspires new thoughts, as these organic rocks seem to change into imaginary forms as do cloud patterns in the sky.

Patterns beneath your feet reinforce the different areas of the Garden. Decorative pavements composed of smooth pebbles, clay tiles and concrete blocks characterize the distinct spaces and create a feeling of much larger spaces. Look carefully as you walk and the richly textured floor patterns will emerge. Each area is unique; the most intricate is that of the Central Courtyard floor. It features a floral pattern composed of thousands of smooth pebbles from river beds in China, as well as broken pieces of white Chinese porcelain bowls, all outlined with bits of clay roof tiles. The variations in these geometric patterns define smaller areas among the rustic rock formations.

◀ *Omnipresent and mystical, these rocks evoke supernatural powers and mysterious beings and draw us into another world.*

▶ *This floor is composed of thousands of smooth pebbles brought from river beds in China, as well as broken pieces of white Chinese porcelain bowls, all outlined with bits of clay tiles.*

▲ *These bold asymmetrical rocks seem to take on imaginary forms.*

The Double Corridor and the Jade Water Pavilion

Intentionally designed to slow down the walk through the Garden, this zigzag colonnade encourages you to savour details along the route. The zigzag design also wards off evil spirits which are thought to travel in straight lines. As you walk through the corridor towards the other parts of the Garden, new vistas continue to emerge as you catch glimpses of what lies ahead through windows and doorways. This also gives you the opportunity to look back and view spaces from different points along the way.

From this double corridor you see the Garden and the adjacent Park through leak windows which deliberately control the vistas. Throughout the Garden there are thirty-six such windows – each with its own lattice design – which literally 'leak' views between spaces. These windows are organized so that they become progressively more geometric as you move towards the scholar's courtyard, primarily a male domain, at the rear of the Garden.

Just before you arrive at the Jade Water Pavilion, you can see a wonderful 'framed view' to the

◄ *Intentionally designed to slow down the walk through the Garden, this zigzag colonnade encourages you to savour details along the route, and also wards off evil spirits which are thought to travel in straight lines.*

Appearing to float on the jade-coloured water, this pavilion sits like a jewel between the Garden and the Park.

west across the courtyard through a lattice-framed window into the Scholar's Study and on to another window, behind which is a 'framed' still life of bamboo and a pointed rock.

From the Jade Water Pavilion you have a new view of the Garden: over the courtyard and back toward the Main Hall, as well as towards the Scholar's Study. Looking to the east you see the Dr. Sun Yat-Sen Park, and beyond the white-washed walls lies Chinatown.

Appearing to float on the jade-coloured water, this pavilion is set like a jewel between the Garden and the Park and is an important stop along our route towards the Scholar's Study. The intricate latticework, upturned eaves, and elegant balustrade provide an aura of grace. Symbolically, the carvings illustrate the qualities of the scholar: the chrysanthemum, a sign of integrity and incorruptibility; bamboo, a symbol of resilience and integrity; plum blos-

soms, signifying perseverance and courage; and the orchid, indicative of moral excellence and a refined, superior man. Notice the northern window paned in pebble glass symbolic of the rice paper which was originally used. This effectively blocks the view beyond and focuses your attention on the beautiful carving of the frame.

Each pavilion provides different vantage points from which to enjoy the Garden. Sit against the Graceful Lady Balustrade, so named for its flowing shape. This shape is only comfortable to lean against when you are facing the view. As you look below, there is the single rose bush – a peculiarly Chinese tribute to a flower they have cherished over the centuries. You will also see the twisted shape of a pine tree – akin to a dragon – and its reflection mirrored in the jade-coloured water.

The cloudy waters which surround you provide reflections of the buildings, rocks and plants.

▲ *A view from The Lookout through the Moongate.*

Thoughts wander as you peer over the balustrade searching for the bottom of the pond. Unlike other garden ponds in Vancouver, this one is intentionally cloudy to intensify the reflections. The jade-green colour also symbolizes tranquility. This effect is created by clay which lines the bottom of these man-made ponds.

From here you leave the pavilion and continue to The Lookout which provides another interlude and an opportunity to look back across the Courtyard to the Main Hall. The Moon Gate entranceway at the rear of The Lookout would normally open into the residence. The planned expansion will lead from here to the new Penjing Garden. Continuing along the zigzag corridor, you pass a small triangular courtyard as you are led to the inner sanctum of the Garden – the Scholar's Study and Courtyard.

▶ *The cloudy waters, jade green in colour, symbolize tranquility and provide reflections of the buildings, rocks and plants.*

The Scholar's Study and Courtyard

At the end of the covered corridor is the traditional Scholar's Study and Courtyard, the quietest and most serene part of the Garden. This secluded area is adjacent to *Szu I Shu Wu*, the Study of the Four Seasons. Emphasizing this theme, behind the Study's northern wall, are the 'three friends of winter' – bamboo, pine and winter-flowering plum – here carefully framed within the lattice-trimmed windows. Further illustrating the theme of opposites is the courtyard which you saw from the Jade Water Pavilion. It contains bamboo accompanied by the pointed rock known as a 'bamboo shoot', which forms the focus of the lattice window on the western wall.

Traditionally, this was where the scholar lived and only men or those closest to the scholar were invited here. The scholar held a unique position in the hierarchy of Chinese culture; it was an honour to serve the court or the government, a privilege reserved for only a few. His residence played an important role in his lifestyle, and consequently, the design of the buildings, furnishings and landscape were visible evidence of his personal taste. The Scholar's Study was built using the same materials and construction techniques as the other buildings throughout the Garden.

These gardens gained popularity among the scholars, nobility and high-ranking government officials, for it was here that they could study and write, compose poetry and music, and paint, all in an environment which encouraged contemplation. In these urban gardens it was possible to commune with nature without leaving the city. Many of the great artistic works were created in these garden retreats. This Scholar's Courtyard contains a sloping walkway leading to a tiny pavilion where artists performed music or recited poetry. This edifice was placed at a higher elevation as a symbol of the scholar's respect for the perfomer, whereas in life outside the garden's walls, the scholar courtier might rank far above the artist.

As you return, the sloping walkway forces you to walk more slowly. This gives you time to notice the interesting perspectives of the small narrow courtyard ahead.

During the Ming dynasty the scholars' gardens flourished, and this is recorded in the writings of the period. An influential treatise published in 1637 under the name of Wen Zhenheng outlined in detail the physical and spiritual characteristics of the scholar's residence. It described the late Ming literati's desire for a particular environment devoid of worldly concerns.

"To live out in the far country is best; next best is to live in the rural areas; next comes the suburbs. Even if we are unable to dwell among the cliffs and valleys and to follow the path of the hermits of old, and we have to settle in city houses, we must ensure that the doors, courtyards, buildings, and rooms are clean and smart, that the pavilions suggest the outlook of a man without worldly cares, and the studies exude the aura of a refined recluse. There should be fine trees and interesting plants, a display of antiquities and books, so that those who live there should forget about age, the guest forget to leave, the visitor to the grounds forget about fatigue."[2]

These private gardens became popular during the Tang and Ming dynasties, and many examples survive in cities along the Yangzi's southern delta. Private gardens were prevalent in cities such as Suzhou, where many scholars settled, and Yangzhou, where many merchants liked to socialize. Gardens in these two communities gradually reflected their owners' desires: the Suzhou scholar's garden was designed as a personal retreat in contrast to the more grandiose design of the Yangzhou businessmen. Both communities were renowned for their gardens; however, it was Suzhou which was fondly called the "city of gardens." Over one hundred of these gardens survive today, and they clearly illustrate the principles of Chinese garden design.

Each scholar played an important role in the design of his own garden. In fact, the intent was not only to design a garden; rather it was to build one. Based upon traditional design and construction techniques, each scholar actively participated in the creation of

▲ *Study of the Four Seasons—by tradition only men and those closest to the scholar were invited here.*

◀ *Symbolically, the most famous group of plants is the trio – the three friends of winter – pine, signifying strength and eternity, bamboo for resiliency amid adversity, and the plum blossom for triumphal rebirth.*

The Scholar's Study and Courtyard, the quietest and most serene part of the Garden.

his own compound.

Although this imitation of the natural world is reflected in the use of standard materials – rocks, water and plants – in classical gardens throughout China, the scholars' gardens were a spiritual interpretation of nature. The importance of the site and the interrelationship between the garden and its surrounding architecture became the main factors in the building of the traditional scholar's garden.

The theme of man's interrelationship with nature is not only limited to the classical garden. Other arts such as painting, poetry and calligraphy also focused on the natural environment. Painting, like garden design, emphasized re-creating nature's essential qualities. The relationship between the artist and the scholar was symbiotic. The scholar searched ancient scrolls and poetry to find inspiration in designing his garden. The artist came into the garden and was moved to express his responses to its beauty with brush or pen. This interplay enabled the artist to exalt the natural world.

The Five Senses

This tranquil classical garden engages all the senses. It is a visual delight as well as an environment enhanced by sound, touch, scent and taste. Often, the focus is on what is seen; however, this is only a beginning. Of course the Garden is a visual feast, from the now familiar elements – rocks, plants, water and buildings – to the unexpected appearances of the blue heron looking for carp in the cloudy waters. This is just a part of our experience. The trickling of water behind the rocks, leaves rustling in the wind, birds chirping and our footsteps on the paving stones all create sounds which are experienced on the walk. Even on a rainy day the Garden is a delight since the sound of rain falling from the roof tiles adds another dimension to our visit. These tiles, fired in China's Imperial Kilns, which were reopened after hundreds of years to supply the Astor Court at the Metropolitan Museum of Art in New

York City, are designed expressly to enhance the water runoff. Known as *di shui* tiles, meaning 'drop of water', they create a curtain of water as the rain splashes off the roof on a rainy day.

The fragrances of spring and summer flowers, pungent pines and fresh air give us a renewed sense of nature in this urban setting. Even on a rainy day the sounds and smells tempt our imagination and help us feel that we have indeed entered into another world.

Consider the different temperatures within the various spaces. Behind the rocks it is cool even on a hot day. The feeling of sunshine on the wooden balustrade of the Jade Water Pavilion is welcome on a crisp winter day. The sense of touch is also present on a more intimate scale as we consider the texture of materials throughout the Garden . . . satin smooth cylindrical pillars of Nan wood tempt the touch, and it is hard to resist running your fingers over the richly carved latticework. The barren rocks in the courtyard pierced with delicate branches of Jasmine present yet another texture.

There is even an opportunity to use our sense of taste when we visit the Garden. From time to time, tea is served in the Main Hall.

Experiencing the Garden as the seasons change adds another dimension – that of time. As the seasons come and go, the foliage changes, bringing different scents and sounds. From blossoming plum trees in spring to a carpet of snow in winter, the Garden is ever-changing.

Although the classical Chinese garden presents a different view of the natural world than a Western garden, it is important to seek an understanding of the symbolism and meaning behind the elements. View this classical Chinese garden as a living art form, look with an open mind and a desire to see beyond the rocks, ponds and plants. A new world will emerge.

The Garden can be appreciated on many different levels – from that of a quiet refuge in the heart of Chinatown to a re-creation of the natural world. Every visitor brings a personal knowledge and understanding to the Garden. Sights and sounds are experienced, and ideally the visitor leaves with a feeling of rejuvenation. Each viewer will see something different. All that is needed is a desire to experience the Garden in a spiritual as well as a physical sense. The Garden as a work of art is a treasure waiting to be discovered.

Endnotes

1. Shen Fu, *Fu-sheng Liu-chi*, p. 92f, as cited in Andrew Plaks, *Archetype and Allegory in the Dream of the Red Chamber*, p. 167.
2. Chu-Tsing Li and James C.Y. Watt, *The Chinese Scholar's Studio: Artistic Life in the Late Ming Period*. (New York: The Asia Society Galleries and Thames and Hudson, 1987) pp. 6–7.

▼ *The roof tiles, known as di shui tiles, meaning 'drop of water,' create a curtain of water as rain splashes off the roof.*

Plants and Botanical Features of the Garden

BY DON VAUGHAN AND JUDY OBERLANDER

Throughout the Garden, plants set the mood of the various areas, and through their symbolism they evoke a unique sense of time and place. Trees and shrubs are used to create a naturalistic landscape and therefore their character and age is particularly important. The delicate branches of the magnolia tree and tufts of mondo grass complement the solid architectural forms and massive rocks which define the Garden's spaces. Carefully planted to evoke small groves, these trees and shrubs bring nature within the Garden walls so that, as in days of old, we can experience the scenic compositions just as the Chinese scholars would have done.

Building a classical Chinese Garden outside of China permitted the designers to be more flexible in the selection of specific plants. Originally the Vancouver design team was concerned with historical accuracy and wanted to use plants which had been used during the Ming dynasty; however, the Suzhou artisans encouraged another approach. Instead of botanical accuracy, their most important consideration was to find plant materials which evoked the appropriate character and which showed signs of their age and maturity. The fact that they were not

◀ *Shady areas along the banks of the pond are ideal for mondo grass and iris.*

specifically Chinese was a minor consideration. Indeed, when the artisans were shown small plant specimens in local nurseries and told that their Latin names corresponded with the plants which would have been used in a Ming dynasty garden, they opted to search for larger local plants which already exhibited the gnarled and twisted character so vital to the Garden's design. The Suzhou artisans also emphasized that this Garden should illustrate its North American character and contain examples of local plant material. This also served to reinforce the merging of the two cultures.

For this reason there is one rosebush – selected by the Suzhou artisans – in the Central Courtyard near the Jade Water Pavilion. Roses, although often considered a Western plant, originated in China and were then transported to England via Persia. Here the rosebush serves as a symbol of both cultures, linking China and the West.

Although China has one of the world's richest collections of ornamental plants and flowers, this is not necessarily reflected in Chinese gardens. This is because the Chinese garden is primarily a landscape composed of walls, rocks, water and architectural elements. Plants fit into this structure in symbolic ways, and are not simply used for their own beauty as we view them in modern Western gardens.[1]

Classical Chinese gardens contained plants known for their mystical and symbolic qualities. Unlike Western gardens in which plants are 'collected', and massed together, plants in this garden are used sparingly and each one is selected for its symbolic meaning and its ability to evoke a natural landscape. This careful selection of plants creates different moods and gives each area a unique character. Wide open spaces in the rockeries are complemented with forceful plants such as the pine and cypress; in contrast, the small rectangular courtyard adjacent to the main hall demands refined and delicate plants such as the wispy bamboo and miniature rhododendron.

Symbolically, the most famous group of plants is the trio — the three friends of winter — pine, bamboo and winter-flowering plum. Carefully planted in the shallow courtyard to the north of the Scholar's Study, these plants possess an importance beyond their presence in the lattice-framed windows. They are associated with human virtues and are often used in painting and poetry as well as gardens. "The solitary pine signifies strength and eternity; the bamboo, resiliency amid adversity; the plum blossom triumphal rebirth."[2]

▲ *The banana plant is symbolic of the heart and soul of the garden.*

Open and closed spaces create a unique feeling in a classical Chinese garden. These spaces are created by the plant materials, the rocks and the architecture. Together they create the continual interplay between solid and void which is visible throughout the Garden. Spaces between the leaves and branches on a tree echo the irregular shapes of the holes in the rocks. Contrasts are continually at play,

and the beauty is that they help us to look at familiar objects in a new way. We must look beyond the individual trees and shrubs and examine how they are placed to create a 'natural' landscape within the Garden walls.

Trees and shrubs also define spaces in the Garden. A group of plants such as the pines and iris in the Central Courtyard define an edge and lead our eyes back into the open courtyard. Other groupings such as the bamboo and pine trees near the grotto give the impression of a secluded mountain hideaway.

Trees serve as screens between different spaces. This helps to hide what lies beyond and increase the viewer's sense of anticipation throughout the Garden. Philosophically this reinforces the desire to make the confined space of the Garden — one-third of an acre — appear larger. Trees also increase the overall sense of space. In contrast to many of the low, horizontal elements in the Garden, tall trees such as the maple and the ginkgo lead the eye up towards the expansive sky. The trees' solid trunks lead to the crown of branches and delicate leaves which give the impression that the courtyards are larger than they really are. On sunny days, the light filtering through the branches creates beautiful patterns on the pavement, once again giving the impression of a larger space.

Trees are used most effectively to change the scale of rock formations and architectural elements. In

▶ *A symbolic collection of the riches, variety and beauty of the earth.*

order to make the central *ting* (pavilion) appear larger, a pine tree was planted on the rock outcropping. Selected for its twisted shape, this tree is reminiscent of those found in nature, often on the side of a rock face as we see here.

Although the location of plants is determined by various factors, including the type of soil, availability of water, orientation toward the sun, the area's sheltered or open character and the proximity of the rocks and buildings, these are conditions which can be controlled as part of the overall design. Accordingly, plants are selected for their suitability to each area, since the desire in building the Garden is to recreate in microcosm the natural landscape. Creating this 'natural' environment is of paramount importance. Shady areas along the banks of the pond are ideal for mondo grasses and iris, whereas sprigs of jasmine peeking out of the rocks on the top of the 'mountain' appear as they do in nature.

Equally important is the placement of the plants. This was evident when Don Vaughan, the Garden's landscape architect, came to plant the mondo grass at the edges of the large rocks. Visually the grass ties the rocks to the pebble mosaics and helps to define the edges of the paved areas. Approaching this task as a Westerner, he proceeded to plant dense clumps of the grass in order to cover the areas of bare soil. Upon seeing the result, the Suzhou artisans began to undo his careful work. Aesthetically, his approach was considered inappropriate for a classical Chinese garden, since it is important to leave areas bare, to see the moss-covered soil and to savour each plant individually. For the artisans, attention to these details was as important as the placement of the large rocks.

The passage of time is essential to our understanding of the Garden. A composition of young plant specimens against a background of grey rocks and stark white walls creates a different impression than that which comes with age and the passage of time. Visible signs of aging are prized; a gnarly old pine tree covered with moss evokes the forces of

◀ *A lone pine tree is selected for its twisted shape, reminding us of those found in nature.*

nature in a tangible way. According to the author Yuan Mei, it is simply "the older the finer."[3]

Throughout the Garden, major rocks are protected by trees. Echoing the familiar *yin* and *yang*, this play of opposites is a motif which reappears throughout the Garden.

Other trees were selected to link landscapes and the surrounding architecture. The ginkgo tree in the central courtyard, for example, complements the light-brown ginkgo latticework of the Jade Water Pavilion and window frames throughout the Garden. Visitors can see both the living tree and ornately carved examples of its wood.

Selecting plants according to their blossom time is very important in a classical garden. This reinforces the importance of seasonal change and heightens the anticipation of spring as the Garden awakens from the winter months.

The Scholar's Courtyard illustrates seasonal change in a more complete manner than other parts of the Garden, since the earliest and latest blooming plants are located here. Each spring, the winter-flowering plum is the first to bloom and the peonies are the last.

The symbolism of viewing the Garden and its plants from different directions during the seasons is important. Looking south across the courtyard one should feel the warm winter sun, whereas in the hot summer weather there should be a cool feeling when one looks towards the north. To the west in the spring one should see the blossoms, and when looking to the east during the autumn harvest festival the full moon should rise through the lattice moon gate.

This Garden, like others in the Ming dynasty tradition, is a variation on a theme. It takes its inspiration from a 2,000-year-old tradition and reinterprets the design principles. There are certain design elements which can be traced to other Suzhou gardens. The Garden's scale is similar to those of the Gardens of the Master of the Fishing Nets and the Unsuccessful Politician in Suzhou. The bamboo and 'bamboo shoot' composition is from the Lion's Grove. This Garden is a composite of the ones from Suzhou and in essence is part of an ongoing tradition, using the same building techniques and similar plant ma-

terials to re-create 'a natural landscape'.

Climatically, Vancouver and Suzhou are quite similar, so many of the plants in the Dr. Sun Yat-Sen Garden are similar to those found in classical gardens of China. Notable exceptions are the lotus and oleander, which do not enjoy the cooler climate. Likewise, the banana – symbolic of the heart and soul of the garden – is kept in a greenhouse during the winter months and then brought to the Garden in warmer weather. It is placed in two areas which contain bamboo – symbolic of the heart and soul of a man – the triangular courtyard near the Scholar's Study and the one between the double corridors leading to the Jade Water Pavilion. Considerations which govern the selection of plant materials include shape, size, age, texture, colour, seasonal changes, foliage density and horticultural requirements. According to Chinese tradition, it is important to find the appropriate shape of tree in nature, so that when it is planted in the Garden it does not appear to have been artificially pruned. For this reason, the search for the desired trees in the Lower

◀ *The Ginkgo, the most ancient of species, is shown in its autumn glory.*

▼ *Chinese beliefs associate some plants with human virtues. The solitary pine signifies strength and eternity.*

Mainland proved to be quite an undertaking. Seeking plant materials with the proper character and age was the goal.

The highly prized winter-flowering plum in the Scholar's Courtyard was located, after much investigation, in a White Rock chicken farm. Happily, a branch, which had been planted and flourished after it had broken off the main tree many years before, was also transported to the Garden and now grows in the shallow courtyard behind the Scholar's Study. The gnarly pine covered with moss which reaches out over the pond in front of The Lookout was found in Vancouver's Queen Elizabeth Park, where it had been carefully tended over the years. Its character and shape – reminiscent of a dragon – was ideal for the Garden. After some negotiation, the Garden was fortunate to obtain this beautiful specimen, since the gardener who had cared for it felt that, like a child leaving home, this tree was indeed being given a good home in the Dr. Sun Yat-Sen Garden.

Endnotes

1. Roy Forster, *Garden Plants and Flowers of China*, p. 1.
2. Roy Forster, *Garden Plants and Flowers of China*, p. 1.
3. Yüan Mei, "Ta-jen Wen Sui-yu" in *Sui-yuan Ch'uan Chi*, p. 56, as cited in Andrew Plaks, *Archetype and Allegory in the Dream of the Red Chamber*, p. 177.

The Development of the Dr. Sun Yat-Sen Classical Chinese Garden

BY JOE WAI

When the Dr. Sun Yat-Sen Classical Chinese Garden was completed in 1986, it appeared to Vancouverites and visitors alike that this was a unique and enchanting if highly improbable project.

How did the first-ever full-scale Chinese classical garden outside Asia get built in Vancouver, British Columbia, at this time in history? What is a Chinese classical garden anyway? Why does it seem so different – and where are the rolling lawns or rose gardens or fountains?

In the West, the notion of a Chinese classical garden is at best unfamiliar. The Japanese garden with its intense clarity of trowelled sand and highly defined elements of singular rock and singular flower had found its way into North America, particularly after the Second World War. But wnat is a Chinese garden? Pagodas and goldfish ponds? Why are there so many buildings?

This unfamiliarity is not new, but neither is the West's fascination with things Chinese, although cultural access into China has been severely limited until the recent decade.

To gain a better perspective, we need to take a longer historical view. In the West, since the times of the ancient Egyptians, gardens have been planned on straight lines and rectangles. The Western garden, based on formal geometric fundamentals, attempts to bring order and symmetry to nature. The rich and the educated cherished great symmetrical palaces overlooking meticulously cultivated and geometric gardens that mirrored the organizing mind of their owners and designers. Versailles in the seventeenth century was a pinnacle example.

In general, one may suggest that gardeners in the West aspire to bring order to their world – an attempt to exert supremacy over nature.

This perhaps is clearly the point of departure, the difference in the Chinese cultural and philosophical outlook as expressed in their gardens. Instead of attempting to control or regulate, the Chinese yearn for harmony with nature, to find a balance between human endeavours and the forces of nature. They long to be partners rather than masters, to ease man's integration with nature, and presumably with the universe.

Such a basic cultural and philosophical outlook is embodied by the Chinese in other major manifestations, such as herbal medicine or acupuncture – seeking a harmony of forces within the human body – as well as classical *feng shui* – seeking a harmony of forces in the built environment within the land, water and sky.

Composed in balance and contradiction with the harsh geometry of Chinese architecture (in turn philosophically based on the Confucian hierarchical societal order), the classical garden is a setting for the imaginative yet practical, profound yet fanciful enjoyment of man's place in the universe.

It can be said that there are three broad categories of Chinese gardens: the imperial gardens on a scale of palatial grandeur; the monastery gardens, the origin of the garden form set in the hills; and the scholar or gentry gardens, which are built primarily in an urban setting of varying size.

The Dr. Sun Yat-Sen Garden is a Suzhou Ming dynasty (A.D. 1368-1644) scholar's garden. Suzhou, a medium-size city, is situated on a system of canals near the mouth of the Yangtze River. It has been renowned for its silk, beautiful maidens and classical gardens for over 2400 years. Here the Scholar's Garden was taken to new levels of refinement in the Song dynasty when over a hundred such fine gardens existed in the city by the year A.D. 1000. In the confines of an urban setting, designers of the scholar's garden through centuries explored, with great care and artistry, ways to maximize the spatial character of the usually limited size of the city sites.

The site of the Dr. Sun Yat-Sen Classical Chinese Garden has played an important role both in the history of Vancouver's China-town, and as an incentive to start the project.

Around the turn of the twentieth century, the block on which the garden rests and the adjacent one to the west formed Chinatown's original site. This block included the many Chi-

The imperial gardens as shown in the scroll above were built on a scale of palatial grandeur whereas the scholar's gardens were generally designed for small urban sites. "Chih Garden."

nese Association buildings, theatres and intra-community commercial outlets. Until 1920, the Great Northern Railway occupied the portion of the land on which the Classical Garden stands today.

This block, then at the edge of False Creek, was gradually filled in. By the 1960s, it became a focus again as the City was planning an elaborate freeway connector system through Chinatown. The historic "Freeway Debates" in City Hall became a turning point in the development of the city and more importantly of Chinatown, as Vancouver rejected the inner city freeway routes. Nevertheless, the very existence of Chinatown was threatened to the core over these protracted debates. With the rejection of the wholesale demolition of urban renewal came urban rehabilitation – an approach which emphasized the value of the existing character and fabric of older neighbourhoods.

In 1972, a Chinese Cultural Centre was formed, and built on this site. The proposal for this project acknowledged the importance of a complex that would be representative of Chinese architecture. This meant the inclusion of a garden, as Chinese architecture is by definition a combination of 'buildings' and 'gardens'. Thus plans, established through an Architectural Competition, included provisions for a Chinese garden, more or less in the eventual location of the Dr. Sun Yat-Sen Park and Classical Garden.

In 1976, discussions on creating a Chinese garden were enthusiastic. However, no one really knew the task involved in building an authentic classical garden. The expertise in design, materials and craftsmanship were seemingly unattainable, and the costs unknown. However, upon visiting gardens in Suzhou and Hangzhou during the previous year, it was discovered that such expertise and authenticity did exist. The question was, how to achieve it?

The financial promise for the Garden began with an unexpected source – $1.5 million of federal funding.

The City of Vancouver established a small but representative Chinese Garden Advisory Committee with Thomas Mah as president. In turn, this committee selected Don Vaughan Associates and Joe Wai Architects as design consultants from a competitive list of local architects and landscape architects in May of 1980.

Shortly thereafter, a development program which would include an authentic classical garden was formulated. Through Dr. Marwyn Samuels, of the University of British Columbia, representatives of the Suzhou Garden Administration (SGA) were invited to Vancouver in June, 1980, to discuss their possible participation in the project. They had just completed the Astor Court – a Ming dynasty schol-

ars study and courtyard – on the second floor of the Metropolitan Museum of New York. The availability of this level of expertise and craftsmanship was inconceivable before the changes in the People's Republic of China in the late 1970s.

The SGA had received many requests for other garden projects during their six months in New York. However, they had decided to pursue the inquiry from Vancouver, as it was on the Pacific Rim, where they wished to establish closer cultural ties. Furthermore, they knew that there was a sizeable Chinese community here, and that the Park/Classical Garden would be a public and non-profit facility.

A Suzhou delegation of five visited Vancouver for a week in June 1980. As well as formulating general principles of cooperation, their two architects, Mr. Zhou Buo Sun and Mr. Wang Zhu Xin began on-site planning with the Canadian design team to develop an authentic, full-scale Ming dynasty classical garden. The Suzhou delegation brought with them a first-hand account and photographs of the Astor Court as positive assurance that this classical expertise and craftsmanship existed.

Unaware and momentarily unconcerned with many of the serious obstacles ahead, the Canadian

LAYOUT OF GARDEN

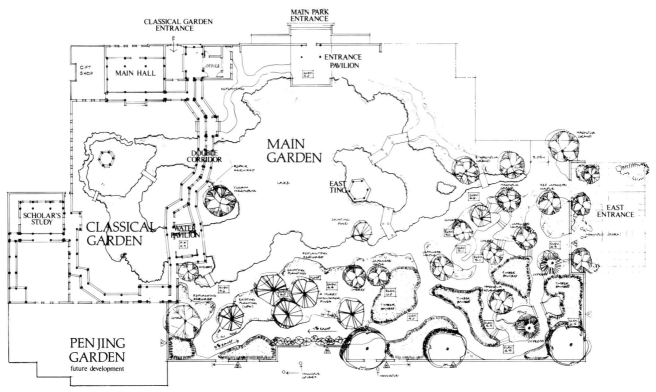

team was truly awestruck at the real possibility of a project that would exceed everyone's fondest expectations. In 1980, China had barely begun opening her doors to the West, and to be able to have her cooperation on such a unique project was most exciting.

The Garden was conceived in two complementary but unequal parts. The greater portion, which would include a large meandering pond, was designed mostly with plant materials, while a smaller portion would be concentrated with pavilions, bridges and false mountains – the building components of the classical garden. The two portions were designed as one, and separated by an appropriately covered bridge or corridor. The entire Garden was to be surrounded by a white-washed wall, similar to the gardens in Suzhou.

Of the development alternatives considered, the one chosen located the Classical Garden portion to the west of the site. This was adjacent to a comparatively quieter street rather than beside a noisier vehicular thoroughfare. Moreover, as Chinese gardens put more value in orientation towards the morning and the noon sun, rather than the afternoon or evening sun, this would put the Classical Garden in the most favourable location within the block.

Traditionally, scholar or gentry gardens were conceived by their owners, scholar poets, who had a sound knowledge of classical gardens and their precedents. In designing their gardens, inspiration would be drawn from the classics, renowned precedents and the site itself. First would come the inspiration – whether from a poem of their own composition depicting an inspired or aspired state of mind; or as an emulation of a revered classical precedent, be it poem, painting or garden. In turn, with the help of the artisan craftsmen, these states of mind would be transformed into physical reality, using traditional elements of rocks, water, walls, windows, pavilions, bridges, terraces and plant material.

The first plans from China included the *Double-sided Corridor* separating the larger portion of the Main Garden (later called the Park) from the approximately 800 square meters of the built-up Classical Garden. This component was inspired by the

several acres of such corridors of the Pavilion of the Gentle Wave Garden Estate in Suzhou, which fronts on a canal.

This corridor would be connected to the south by a *Water Pavilion*, which was re-created almost intact from another of the famous Suzhou Gardens – the Garden of the Humble Civil Servant.

Two of the *rock formations* follow the emphasis on singular rock mass in the *Lingering Garden*.

However, the size and the general character of the Dr. Sun Yat-Sen Classical Garden was inspired by a relatively small but exquisite garden in Suzhou – the Garden of the Master of the Fishing Nets, where a central water body is surrounded and enhanced by several pavilions, varying in size and purpose. The two principal pavilions – the *Main Reception Hall* and the *Scholar's Study* – are derived from similar pavilions in that Garden.

Upon reception of the preliminary plans, work would begin on the Park to complement the Classical Garden. The site would be surrounded by a simple but dramatic three- to four-metre wall. A central Moon Gate would form the main entrance to the Park, while to the west, a quiet but intriguing separate entrance would give access to the Classical Garden.

The Park itself was to be composed of a large pond, an island with bridges, one small pavilion and considerable plant material.

A delegation from Vancouver was sent to Suzhou to further develop plans. The logistics of preparing the materials in various centres around Suzhou and the eventual travel of the fifty-two artisans to Vancouver were complicated and would require one year of advance notice after signing the agreement prior to construction.

The visit was invaluable – it was possible to see all of the gardens discussed in design sessions, and to view on the sites the various elements and components proposed. It was now abundantly clear that education on the classical garden had only just begun.

In terms of craftsmanship, it was most reassuring to see it in progress in Suzhou, and to know that such expertise truly existed.

The return from this most fruitful visit to Suzhou produced a very real and sobering thought. The project really had no funding as yet. The overall cost was projected to be in excess of six million dollars for both the Park and Classical Garden.

Just as timely and important as the Suzhou Garden Administration's participation in the project, the summer of 1981 brought forth the patrons of the Garden. Dr. David Lam, eventually lieutenant-governor of this province, was a philanthropist with a vision. He pledged one million dollars for the construction of the Classical Garden. This established the credibility of the project's capital campaign. Furthermore, several of the most prominent citizens of Vancouver became involved, and began a five-year tireless campaign of fundraising and the establishment of a non-profit organization, which would oversee the emergent complex project.

In the fall of 1981, the Dr. Sun Yat-Sen Classical Garden Society was formed, with specific responsibility for the Classical Garden portion of the project, while the City of Vancouver, through its Board of Parks and Recreation, would continue with the Park.

The composition of the Society was vital from the start, and it exemplifies the spirit which the project symbolizes – the cooperation between China and Canada. A significant number of the first trustees of the Society (as they continue to be today) were not of Chinese origin. Together with the Chinese Canadian members, they were able to reach out and promote the project within and outside the Chinese community in Vancouver, making this a truly multicultural effort.

Furthermore, to show its support, the City had appointed a liaison alderman and a parks commissioner to sit on the Board of Trustees. Their work in early 1982 was most difficult, as an economic recession was just beginning.

Meanwhile, City support was sought to proceed with the first phases of the overall site. With the fate of the Classical Garden in question, the City acted to proceed with phase two of the Park, and constructed the bridges, the islands, the main pond, the north wall and the main gate, in order to establish a real

proof that the project had not been abandoned. As a result the Park was completed in the fall of 1983.

While the Park was in construction, capital funding for the Classical Garden received significant encouragement from the provincial government. A grant eventually totalling $1.3 million was given on condition that the project be completed prior to the opening of a world's fair, Expo '86, in April.

Mr. Wang, chief architect, came with the Jiangsu-Suzhou delegation to sign the contract with the Garden Society under President S.K. Lee. All involved were able to further their collaboration on the detailed design of the project. Prior to their visit, the delegation had sent preliminary construction drawings for review. The plans were adapted to conform to the Canadian and Vancouver building codes. Among a number of issues involved were stringent requirements for seismic design, as Vancouver is situated in a high earthquake risk zone. In pavilion design, this required the replacement of the brick construction between columns by reinforced concrete. Another issue was the Chinese structural timber. A sample shipment was received and tested in local laboratories. It was discovered that the Chinese fir has similar structural properties to the Canadian pine. In addition, a handful of reinforcing steel spikes were added to the primarily mortise-and-tenon approach of Chinese classical timber design.

During this week of collaboration, a number of technical questions were resolved. These included the approach used to hide the wiring within the larger wood beams and the use of radiant heating under the clay brick tile flooring of the pavilions. It was impressive that all efforts were acutely directed to maintain authenticity, while accommodating local requirements and technology.

By the spring of 1984, time was running out if the provincial government's deadline was to be met. Under the Society's new president, Ron Shon, a massive capital campaign was launched in the summer of 1984, which was remarkably successful. An eleventh-hour request was sent to Suzhou regarding schedule and funding programs. The Suzhou municipal government generously agreed to reduce the costs by a further $200,000, and the project was at long last approved for construction by the Society in November 1984.

All of a sudden, all previous preparations had to be compressed, to accommodate an immediate start in January 1985, with the Suzhou artisans arriving in March.

The logistics were considerable: transport of the artisans, securing their local accommodation and shipping of the materials to Vancouver. Furthermore, considerable site preparations by local contractors had to be arranged. Despite the overwhelming amount of work required over a short period of time, the seemingly endless uncertainties were over. This was the beginning of the realization of the project, which would exceed all expectations.

The construction started in January 1985, with the installation of timber piles and concrete ground beams as a part of the seismic requirement.

With the imminent arrival of the fifty-two artisans from Suzhou, the search for appropriate accommodation for them became imperative. Among the number of options available, a nearby hotel was selected, although renovations were required before occupancy.

A carpenter wearing a rattan "hard-hat" puts a timber in place.

Then an unexpected problem arose. As a number of the artisans were older, there had been a delay in their health clearance to enter Canada. Because of the tight and economical travel arrangements, this had the makings of a major disaster to the schedule and the budget.

Through the office of the local member of parliament, the Honorable Pat Carney, the safe processing period for the artisans was minimized and they eventually arrived in three groups: in March, April and in June. Later, more assistance was given to resolve duty issues on the custom-made materials. As well a further and badly needed capital grant for the project was gifted by the federal government.

Meanwhile, with the arrival of the advance team, joint coordination of the project began. Weekly schedules were established on construction progress, and twice-a-week sessions were held on logistics of materials and personnel – both local and those imported from Suzhou.

The materials arrived in seventy sea-going steel containers, and were composed of 965 custom-made wood packing cases. Arrangements were made with Expo '86 to store the materials and construct a temporary workshop on an adjacent vacant site.

The first construction work by the artisans began in April when the second group arrived. This group included the masons, and they quickly began installing the granite pavilion bases after making laborious refinements with hand tools on the reinforced concrete floors and ground beams, which had been constructed by the local contractor.

Within twenty-five days of their arrival, the first wall was erected, and very shortly after that the wood structural frame with its hand-made joinery was completed for the Main Hall. The first pavilion began to take form.

The official name for these artisans was the Suzhou Classical Garden Technical Expert Team. It was led by Mr. Liu Yan Fu, who was also the director of the SGA. His deputy leader was Chen Yao Yuan, a master craftsman with years of experience in the field, who acted as the main supervisor on site for all the different teams of artisans. The teams, ranging from groups of four to eight, were divided by trades: the masons, the heavy timber carpenters, the finishing carpenters, the tilers (clay brick roof tiles and leak windows), the paving tilers (flooring, decorative edges and paving patterns), the painters and carvers and the false mountain rockery artisans. Each team worked under a master craftsman, much like the old Western guild system.

When the 'false mountain', or rockery, team finally arrived with the third and last group of artisans, it was led by a master craftsman in his seventies. Their task was the most spectacular, as they were to assemble the endless number of eroded limestone pieces into highly exciting standing rock-sculptures in specific locations in the Garden. Their more time-consuming task was the building of the central 'mountain' with these rocks, which took the six of them six whole months. These rocks are genuine Tai Hu rocks from the famous lake near Suzhou. The Chinese have been using these picturesque, eroded limestone rocks for centuries to decorate their gardens as well as to represent landforms. The placement of these rocks was entirely the responsibility of the 'false mountain' master craftsman. A main issue in the beginning was how to transport the heavy pieces within the site. After some consideration of available mechanized cranes, the team decided to return to traditional methods of bamboo and manual labour for horizontal transport, and tripod and chain for vertical transport.

The carpenters assembled and fitted the pre-made pieces with great expertise, using mostly traditional tools and equipment that must have been centuries old in design. The hammers, saws and other utensils, unlike their contemporary Western counterparts, seemed like art objects themselves. The wood used in the Garden all came from China – Chinese fir for most structural members, camphor for the curved rafters, ginkgo for the delicate screens. The principal columns, four each in the Main Hall and the Scholar's Study, were made of Nan wood, which has been the traditional species for such use in China for over 2000 years. Nan was also used for coffins of the wealthy. This double demand for the wood, which is native only to West-

ern China, has caused it to become an endangered species. It was fortunate that eight columns were obtainable, residue of the special order for the New York project.

While teams of artisans had their specific responsibilities, the day-to-day scheduling and coordination was done by Mr. Wang and Mr. Chen. Mr. Wang had the added responsibility of coordinating the artisans' work with the local designers and con-

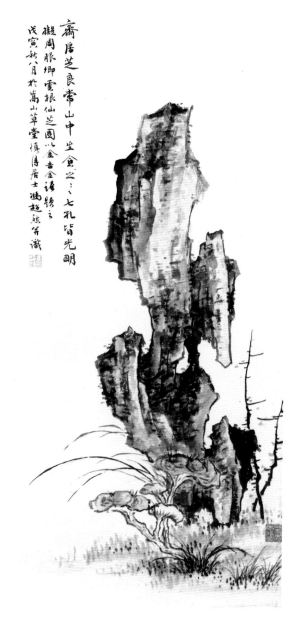

The Suchou craftsmen assembled the endless number of eroded limestone pieces in highly exciting rock sculptures, in keeping with the style of this classic scroll.

Using traditional tools, the craftsmen are assembling the lattice work window frames.

tractor. Frequent and regular meetings were held where progress and projections were charted on a weekly basis. More importantly, problems were resolved. As in any construction project, they were ever present. However, difficulties arising from this project were often unusual if not unique. The attitude and approach of resolving them always remained the same, whether they involved local forces or the artisans: "It is a mutual problem, and we shall solve it together by cooperation," as opposed to the confrontational attitudes that sometimes prevail between architect and contractor on construction sites.

As the construction took place in a relatively visible site, onlookers watched with increasing curiosity, as the various classical architectural elements took form along with the 'false mountain' rockery. Aside from the obvious, there existed a curious sense of something extraordinary taking place . . . a sense of involved fascination. This attachment also was found in our local construction crew. At first they were wary of the number and the method of the artisans. After a month of working side by side, they began to understand the rhythm, ingenuity and craftsmanship of these artisans who used such ancient-looking tools. Their cooperation on-site became easy and intense. Although the artisans had a very capable translator, language was no longer an important issue as they converged in collaboration.

This attentive collaboration was certainly needed when the teams began to combine their two approaches in attempting to pour concrete between the perfectly erect and finely finished wood columns already in place. Artisans from both sides offered many suggestions: how to protect the columns from wet concrete, how to control the weight and pressure by pouring a metre depth at a time. Although this is not advanced technology, the process of resolving such problems was most satisfying to all involved – and so were the results.

One curious incident occurred early in construction as the Chinese artisans began to work in their traditional rattan 'hard' hats, and canvas work boots. The local Workers Compensation Board inspector was unimpressed and served a stop-work order that their equipment be changed immediately. After many discussions with the artisans, who stated that these were always adequate for them, they relented, and took the Canadian plastic hard hats and work boots. The question put to them was: "If a brick falls on the rattan hat, would it be able to offer sufficient protection?" Their answer was, "Depends on how high the brick is falling from."

Seventy percent of the tree and plant material traditionally found in a Suzhou classical garden was fortunately found locally. With the strict import regulations, it would have been most difficult otherwise. The other thirty percent was substituted with similar families of plants where deemed appropriate. However, at the end of a six-month search in local nurseries, a significant number of the larger important trees could not be found. In classical garden design, it is not only important to have the appropriate species at the right location, but also the appropriate shape. The shape or form desired is often 'crooked' or in a form other than what we tend to grow here – which is usually straight up and down. After much searching, several large pine trees and green maples were found in nearby Strathcona Neighbourhood Park. Many discussions, including door-to-door consultations with adjacent residents and the Board of Parks and Recreation, were required before an exchange of trees was possible.

The names of the pavilions and the scripts over the adjacent designated places are integral parts of the character of the Garden. They evoke a state of

mind and set a tone or give a meaning to that particular component or place. Calligraphy, an established art in classical China, plays an important part in the Garden's character. When the design drawings were nearing completion, the SGA was asked to help name the pavilions and provide the appropriate scripts. Four different scripts, including the ancient pre-Han dynasty script, were chosen, in order to provide diversity in the calligraphy itself. Some of the characters were written in Suzhou, and the remainder were written locally by a Vancouver master, Mr. Leung Shak Fung. The characters were traced carefully onto a mold from which the characters were carved out of brick tiles, and painted in place.

As diversity is desirable, we were fortunate to have the main title of the Park "Sun Yat-Sen Public Garden" written by Madame Sun Yat-Sen herself, prior to her final illness. It was an unexpected but pleasant result of a request which was made to her intermediaries in Beijing in 1981.

Life far away from home for a whole year may be a hardship for many, but the Suzhou artisans appeared to adjust relatively well. Approximately a quarter of the team had been in New York to work on the Astor Court five years earlier, and a few others also had been abroad in Japan on assignment. However, for the majority, it was their first trip to a strange land. We had billeted them in an old hotel four blocks from the construction site. The hotel had been renovated to accommodate a large dining area, including a kitchen equipped for large-scale Chinese cooking. They brought with them their own cook and his assistant, thus providing a constant in their diet.

They preferred to work with available daylight,

▲ *This detail of the ceiling in the main hall shows the complicated joinery which the artisans so skillfully fashioned with materials, tools, and skills little changed in a thousand years.*

and started early in summer at 6:30 A.M., returning to their hotel at 11:30 for lunch and a rest. They returned at 2:30 and often stayed until 7:00 P.M. In the winter, the starting time was as late as 8:00 A.M., and work finished by 4:30 in the afternoon. Most of the time this routine was in force six days a week.

At work, their attitude was exemplary: diligent, cooperative and enthusiastic. Under the benevolent leadership of Mr. Liu and the capable coordination of Mr. Chen and Mr. Wang, problems big and small were usually quickly resolved.

On Sundays, the Society trustees and volunteers planned many outings for them. There were bus trips to places of interest in Vancouver and surrounding areas, particularly gardens and parks. Organizations in Chinatown, particularly the Chinese Cultural Centre, held receptions and dinners for them. There were a number of festive events, some arranged by the Society and others by the artisans to mark the seasons and the progress of the project. In late September, they staged a mid-project celebration coinciding with the mid-autumn festival, and treated thirty Society trustees and guests to an elaborate dinner at their own modest facilities. The Society in turn invited them to a special Christmas party, complete with an introduction to Santa Claus. Table tennis was highly popular with the Chinese, and the table provided for them at the hotel was in constant use during leisure hours. They staged tournaments on their days of rest, and included several new friends during the New Year holiday celebrations.

Towards the latter part of the construction, the Society was bolstered by new trustees and volunteers, now preparing in earnest for the completion and operation of the Garden. During this period, new requirements, such as a larger office area and a gift shop, were added. As late additions to the complex, these two small areas were designed in wood construction, and built by local forces. The exterior, such as the roof, however, was finished by the artisans to match the other pavilions.

Much preparation was required before the opening on April 24, 1986. The tireless trustees, a dedicated young staff and a growing number of volunteers who eventually became guides for the Garden,worked in parallel to the construction. As in all other phases of the work, the way was found for a successful opening. As the dignitaries from both Canadian and Chinese governments officiated at the proceedings, the unseasonable cold April rain could not dampen the spirits of all who were fortunate to be involved in this extraordinary experience.

At last with the opening came the visitors, and with the visitors came an increasingly widespread enjoyment and awareness of the first authentic Suzhou Scholar's Garden outside of Asia. Its realization seemed to us a frozen moment of crystallized harmony in a generally chaotic world. It appeared that all those who had been introduced to the project became enchanted. Through this came the faith and the energy to collectively create the Dr. Sun Yat-Sen Classical Chinese Garden.

The dedication and the generosity of so many on both sides of the Pacific have made the Garden a living symbol of international cooperation. In Vancouver, this spirit of cooperation has bridged cultural enclaves. The Chinese Canadian community has been joined by Vancouverites at large. By their joint involvement, each has contributed something to a

The fine workmanship of the Chinese craftsmen is beautifully exhibited in this column detail from the interior of the main hall.

larger whole. It may be called the spirit of multiculturalism or perhaps the spirit of the classical garden. It is here that individuals find their places in nature and strive to live in a balance of harmony and contrast with each other and with the ever-changing elements of the universe.

"Expectation of Full-Blooming" Chinese Wisteria

The Art of Penjing

BY JUDY OBERLANDER

Classical Chinese gardens often contain arrangements of miniature trees and rockeries known as *penjing*. These creations of carefully pruned trees and rocks are small-scale renditions of the natural landscape. They are often referred to as living sculptures or as three-dimensional poetry. Their artistic composition captures the spirit of nature and distinguishes them from potted plants. Quite small in size, these miniature landscapes include trees which are frequently over a hundred years old. Like the plants in the Garden, they have been carefully selected and tended so that they develop into twisted and gnarled shapes reminiscent of their full-size counterparts in the wild.

Historically, *penjing* can be traced back to seventh-century China. This is documented in a seventh- century fresco found in the paved path which led towards Prince Zhang Huai's tomb in Shaanxi Province. It depicts a court maiden holding a miniature landscape. This fresco, which was excavated by archaeologists in 1972, is probably the world's oldest visual evidence of *penjing*.

Over the next 1200 years, *penjing* developed into a highly skilled art form. Subsequently, it was transported to Japan, where it became known as the art of *bonsai*. The Japanese refined this art form and over the years it has become known throughout the world.

As an art form, *penjing* is an extension of the garden, since it enables an artist to recreate in miniature parts of the natural landscape. Using artificially dwarfed trees and shrubs, these arrangements are created in special trays or pots which are placed on ornately carved wooden stands. Often, rocks and porcelain figurines are added to give the proper scale as part of the natural scenery.

There are two main types of *penjing*, classified according to their materials: *Shan Dan Penjing*, or rockery *penjing*; and *Susun Penjing*, or stump penjing.

In turn these materials can be used to design arrangements of single trees or more complex ones which convey the sense of an entire landscape. In all cases, their beauty lies in the total composition, from the subtle shapes of the foliage to the stand which supports the tray in which the work of art will grow over more than a century. Antique pots, which are treasures in themselves, are sometimes used for these arrangements.

Like the gardens, these miniature landscapes are designed to convey landscapes experienced from various viewpoints – a close-up view, a medium range view or a panorama.

The strategic placement of plants and rocks in the pots gives the impression of scale. This is reinforced by the careful pruning of the trees in relation to the rocks, pavilions and figurines to give the desired impression of either an intimate or a vast landscape. The same design principles which apply to the Garden are used in the art of *penjing*. Although they represent different scales, they seek the same recreation of the natural world. Both convey the sense of time and space found in nature. Indeed, the passage of time is very much a part of *penjing* and despite the diminutive size of the trees, they change with the seasons, becoming gnarled and bent over just as those in the Garden do.

Penjing is often used indoors as part of a garden's overall design, since it reiterates the landscape features found outside. *Penjing* pots grace pavilions, private studies and living rooms, as well as public buildings. They are either free-standing elements within the gardens or are placed on furniture such as a table or bookshelf. Sometimes a lattice display stand is built which adds particular prominence to the *penjing* specimen and exemplifies the interplay between architecture and nature.

▼ *Different scales can be created in the same size of container to convey close-up, medium range or panoramic views*

A display of *penjing* must complement its surroundings in a harmonious manner. The background should be simple so as to permit the viewer to focus on the display pieces. Plain backgrounds such as the stark white garden walls or a dark wood door are attractive backdrops for *penjing*.

The Dr. Sun Yat-Sen Garden is most fortunate to be the recipient of a splendid *penjing* collection from Dr. Wu Yee Sun, a Hong Kong banker. This world-renowned collector has donated part of his collection to this Garden and part to the Montreal Botanical Garden. As an integral component of a classical garden, this *penjing* collection will add a new dimension to the Dr. Sun Yat-Sen Garden.

The cultivation of these miniature plants is a highly developed art form. Pruning the branches and the roots results in the growth of stunted trees which are reminiscent of the full-scale and ancient trees found in nature.

A wide variety of plant materials – some 160 species in all – are used in *penjing*. These are selected for their longevity, resiliency to transplanting, slender branches and small leaves. Those with picturesque trunks and attractive blossoms are the most highly prized.

There are a variety of ways in which the plants are selected and then cultivated into *penjing*. Some trees are found as small stunted specimens growing in rock crevices or along the banks of streams. These can be collected after they become dormant and then carefully pruned to control their growth and encourage a picturesque silhouette. The most popular plant materials which are found in this way in-

clude pine, elm, bamboo, trident maple, cape jasmine, Chinese holly, hawthorn and wisteria.

Another group of plants for miniature gardens cannot be found in nature and are therefore artificially propagated. This means that they are grown from seed, are cut from a branch of an older tree or root, or are grafted. In all cases, great care is taken to produce an almost endless variety of miniature trees to reflect their natural counterparts.

Penjing trees are shaped according to certain characteristics. There are straight trunks which are topped with a crown of branches; those which overhang the pot in a way which recalls a tree on top of a cliff; double trunks on a slant which imitate the wind-blown trees in nature; withered, ancient-looking trunks which are crowned by foliage, and a connected root which has a series of trunks all growing out of an exposed root. As each specimen is shaped – first the trunk, then the main branches, followed by the smaller ones – its inherent characteristics are embellished. The result is that these artistic forms mirror, on a much smaller scale, the same species found inside and outside the garden walls.

Penjing trees come in different sizes: small, 10-40 centimetres high; medium, 40-80 centimetres, and large, 80-150 centimetres. Height is measured from the crown of the tree to the surface of the tray or pot and the length is considered the length of the tray. Despite these diminutive measurements, the small trees change little from year to year. Although their leaves and blossoms regenerate annually, the overall form of each miniature landscape remains unchanged.

Rocks are an essential component of *penjing*. As in the Garden, rocks represent mountainous landscapes and their presence is an integral part of the composition. Many different kinds of rocks can be used for *penjing*. There are soft rocks such as pumice; *shaji* – grey sedimentary rocks formed of mud and sandy soil; and *haimu* – formed by deposits of sea shells in shallow coastal waters. Hard rocks are also used, including those highly prized ones from Lake Tai in Jiangsu Province; *qi*, or 'strange-looking' rocks with a horizontal grain; *fupi*, or axinite rocks with vertical grains; stalactites from limestone

caves as well as dark-grey stalagmites. The softer rocks can be carved into various shapes and they readily absorb water, which encourages the growth of mosses and plants on their surfaces. Although hard rocks are difficult to carve, their eroded shapes and natural colours make them ideal for *penjing*.

Rocks placed within these miniature landscapes often recall the cliffs and precipices of China's mountainous regions. In order to achieve this, the initial rock selection and their asymmetrical placement are crucial. To create a lively composition is a challenge and one which requires artistic judgement, knowledge and experience. Rocks – often seen as static and solid – can be arranged to give the impression of movement, and when partially hidden by trees and plants they encourage the viewer's imagination. Like the gardens, *penjing* arrangements often include rare Lake Taï rocks which add to the symbolism of a miniaturized garden.

As in landscape painting, the creation of a miniature landscape requires a careful planning process. The artist must visualize the total work in order to arrive at a unified assembly of rocks and plants reminiscent of the natural landscape. This is particularly important so that proportions are accurate, the principles of perspective are respected, and the various elements harmonize with one another. In effect, *penjing* is a three-dimensional painting and, therefore, the experience of viewing it from various angles should also contribute to its beauty.

Endnotes

1. Hu Yunhua, *Penjing: The Chinese Art of Miniature Gardens.* (Beaverton, Oregon: Timber Press in cooperation with the American Horticultural Society, 1982) p. 7.
2. Chen Lifang and Yu Sianglin, *The Garden Art of China.* (Portland, Oregon: Timber Press, 1986) p. 149.
3. Frances Ya-sing Tsu, *Landscape Design in Chinese Gardens.* (New York: McGraw-Hill Book Company, 1988) p. 152.
4. Hu Yunhyua, *Penjing: The Chinese Art of Miniature Gardens.* (Beaverton, Oregon: Timber Press in cooperation with the American Horticultural Society, 1982) pp. 79–84.

Dr. Sun Yat-Sen: Profile of a Leader

Known as the 'Father of Modern China,' Dr. Sun Yat-Sen was an important figure in the development of the Republic of China. He was internationally recognized by members of all political affiliations for his central role in the history of modern China. As the first non-gentry leader of a political movement, he sought to bring democracy to his country during the early years of the twentieth century.

His connection with Vancouver is significant since he visited several times on fundraising missions to support the revolution which ultimately overturned the monarchy. Born into a peasant family in Cuiheng village, Xiangshan County (now Zhongshan City) in Guangdong Province on November 12, 1866, he was educated abroad and therefore exposed to Western thought at any early age. Although he became a doctor, he left his medical career in order to devote himself to the cause of democracy. As China's first professional revolutionary he travelled around the world to promote the pro-democracy movement and to raise funds for his work.

During his visits to Vancouver in 1910 and 1911, it is said that Dr. Sun Yat-Sen stayed in a building at the corner of Pender and Carrall. This building,

built c. 1901, stands today as a good example of the merging of Eastern and Western architecture.

As a symbol of modern China, Dr. Sun Yat-Sen became a hero and is remembered as *Guo Fu*, Father of the Country. He died on March 12, 1925.

Naming the Garden in his honour is a fitting tribute to a man who dedicated his life to helping China develop ties with the rest of the world. Simultaneously, he sought to make the world more aware of China and its ancient civilization. Indeed, the promoting of cultural understanding was an important part of his work and is central to the creation of this Garden in Vancouver.

Dr. Sun Yat-Sen and the Garden's cultural importance are commemorated in a pair of scrolls which are hung from time to time in the Main Hall. In translation they read, "An exquisite garden built in Vancouver to commemorate the accomplishments of the past ages" and "An elegant view resembling that of Suzhou to proclaim the greatness of Chinese culture."

Madam Sun Yat-Sen is also represented in the Garden; a carved version of her calligraphy can be found above the entrance to the Park. This stone plaque, which translates as 'Dr. Sun Yat-Sen Park', welcomes visitors as they pass through the Moon Gate.

Chronology

Neolithic	c. 8000-2000 B.C.
Xia	c. 2000-1523 B.C.
Shang	1523-1028 B.C.
Zhou	1027-256 B.C.
Western Zhou	1027-256 B.C.
Eastern Zhou	771-256 B.C.
Qin	221-206 B.C.
Han Dynasty	206 B.C. - AD 220
Western Han	206 B.C. - AD 9
Xin Dynasty	9-23
Eastern Han	25-220
Three Kingdoms	221-265
Western Dynasties	265-589
Western Jin	265-317
Eastern Jin	317-420
Liu Song	420-479
Southern Qi	479-502
Liang	502-557
Chen	557-589
Northern Dynasties	
Northern Wei	386-534
Eastern Wei	534-550
Western Wei	535-556
Northern Qi	550-577
Northern Zhou	557-581
Sui Dynasty	581-618
Tang Dynasty	618-907
Five Dynasties	907-960
Liao Dynasty	907-1125
Song Dynasty	960-1279
Northern Song	960-1127
Southern Song	1127-1279
Jin Dynasty	1115-1234

Yuan Dynasty	1280-1368
Ming Dynasty	1368-1644
Qing Dynasty	1644-1912
Republic of China	1912-1949
People's Republic of China	1949-

Since there are several chronological systems currently in use, individual authors have chosen to observe slightly different chronologies in their essays.

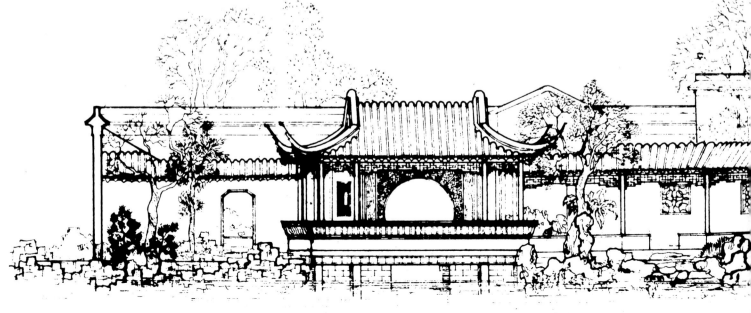